Apollos

Paul's Social Network: Brothers and Sisters in Faith
Bruce J. Malina, Series Editor

Apollos

Paul's Partner or Rival?

Patrick J. Hartin

For Loretta:
In Friendship
Patrick
May 2009

A Michael Glazier Book

LITURGICAL PRESS
Collegeville, Minnesota

www.litpress.org

A Michael Glazier Book published by Liturgical Press

Cover design by Ann Blattner. *Saint Paul*, fresco fragment, Roma, 13th century.

1   2   3   4   5   6   7   8   9

Library of Congress Cataloging-in-Publication Data

Hartin, P. J. (Patrick J.)
   Apollos : Paul's partner or rival? / Patrick J. Hartin.
     p. cm.
   "A Michael Glazier book."
   Includes bibliographical references and index.
   ISBN 978-0-8146-5263-3 (pbk.)
   1. Apollos (Biblical figure)   2. Paul, the Apostle, Saint—Friends and associates.   I. Title.

BS2452.A66H37 2009
226.6'092—dc22   2008050213

To my students, past and present,
who continue to challenge and inspire me.

CONTENTS

Preface   ix

Acknowledgments   xi

References to Apollos in the New Testament   xiii

Introduction
   Who Is Apollos?   1

Chapter 1
   Apollos: "Sense of the Self"   7

Chapter 2
   Apollos: Embedded in a Collectivistic Culture   20

Chapter 3
   **Apollos and Corinth:
   First-Generation Testimony**   46

Chapter 4
   **Apollos of Alexandria:
   Third-Generation Recollections**   68

Conclusion
Apollos: Partner of Paul 102

Notes 110

Bibliography 118

Index of Persons and Subjects 124

Scripture and Ancient Authors Index 134

PREFACE

Human beings are embedded in a set of social relations. A social network is one way of conceiving that set of social relations in terms of a number of persons connected to one another by varying degrees of relatedness. In the early Jesus group documents featuring Paul and coworkers, it takes little effort to envision the apostle's collection of friends and friends of friends that is the Pauline network.

This set of brief books consists of a description of some of the significant persons who constituted the Pauline network. For Christians of the Western tradition, these persons are significant ancestors in faith. While each of them is worth knowing by themselves, it is largely because of their standing within that web of social relations woven about and around Paul that they are of lasting interest. Through this series we hope to come to know those persons in ways befitting their first-century Mediterranean culture.

Bruce J. Malina
Creighton University
Series Editor

ACKNOWLEDGMENTS

I should like to acknowledge my appreciation for the assistance given me in the production of this manuscript. In particular I am indebted to Bruce J. Malina and the members of the Catholic Biblical Association Task Force of the Social-Scientific Methodology who initiated me into this methodology for understanding the New Testament. My enormous thanks go as well to Andrew Jorgenson for his meticulous and diligent work as research assistant during every stage of the development of this manuscript. His assistance was invaluable. I wish to thank as well Peter Henggeler for his methodological construction of the Index of Persons and Subjects found at the end of the book. Finally, I should like to thank the editors of Liturgical Press for all their assistance as well, especially Lauren L. Murphy, Mary Stommes, Colleen Stiller, and Hans Christoffersen.

REFERENCES TO APOLLOS
IN THE NEW TESTAMENT

A. First Letter of Paul to the Corinthians:

Testimony of Paul and His Coworker Sosthenes to Apollos

1 Corinthians 1:10-17

[10]Now I appeal to you, brothers and sisters, by the name of our Lord Jesus Christ, that all of you be in agreement and that there be no divisions among you, but that you be united in the same mind and the same purpose.

[11]For it has been reported to me by Chloe's people that there are quarrels among you, my brothers and sisters.

[12]*What I mean is that each of you says, "I belong to Paul," or "I belong to Apollos," or "I belong to Cephas," or "I belong to Christ."*

[13]Has Christ been divided? Was Paul crucified for you? Or were you baptized in the name of Paul?

[14]I thank God that I baptized none of you except Crispus and Gaius,

[15]so that no one can say that you were baptized in my name.

[16](I did baptize also the household of Stephanas; beyond that, I do not know whether I baptized anyone else.)

[17]For Christ did not send me to baptize but to proclaim the gospel, and not with eloquent wisdom, so that the cross of Christ might not be emptied of its power.

1 Corinthians 3:1-9

¹And so, brothers and sisters, I could not speak to you as spiritual people, but rather as people of the flesh, as infants in Christ.

²I fed you with milk, not solid food, for you were not ready for solid food.

Even now you are still not ready,

³for you are still of the flesh. For as long as there is jealousy and quarreling among you, are you not of the flesh, and behaving according to human inclinations?

⁴*For when one says, "I belong to Paul," and another, "I belong to Apollos," are you not merely human?*

⁵*What then is Apollos? What is Paul? Servants through whom you came to believe, as the Lord assigned to each.*

⁶*I planted, Apollos watered, but God gave the growth.*

⁷So neither the one who plants nor the one who waters is anything, but only God who gives the growth.

⁸The one who plants and the one who waters have a common purpose, and each will receive wages according to the labor of each.

⁹For we are God's servants, working together; you are God's field, God's building.

1 Corinthians 3:21-23

²¹So let no one boast about human leaders. For all things are yours,

²²*whether Paul or Apollos or Cephas or the world or life or death or the present or the future—all belong to you,*

²³and you belong to Christ, and Christ belongs to God.

1 Corinthians 4:1-7

¹Think of us in this way, as servants of Christ and stewards of God's mysteries.

²Moreover, it is required of stewards that they be found trustworthy.

³But with me it is a very small thing that I should be judged by you or by any human court.

I do not even judge myself.

⁴I am not aware of anything against myself, but I am not thereby acquitted.

It is the Lord who judges me.

⁵Therefore do not pronounce judgment before the time, before the Lord comes, who will bring to light the things now hidden in darkness and will disclose the purposes of the heart. Then each one will receive commendation from God.

⁶*I have applied all this to Apollos and myself for your benefit, brothers and sisters, so that you may learn through us the meaning of the saying,* "Nothing beyond what is written," so that none of you will be puffed up in favor of one against another.

⁷For who sees anything different in you?

What do you have that you did not receive?

And if you received it, why do you boast as if it were not a gift?

1 Corinthians 16:12

Now concerning our brother Apollos, I strongly urged him to visit you with the other brothers, but he was not at all willing to come now. He will come when he has the opportunity.

(Other texts read: "it was not at all God's will for him *to come now")*

B.   The Acts of the Apostles

(from the Third-Generation Pauline Tradition)
Recollections about Apollos from Luke

Acts 18:24-28

²⁴Now there came to Ephesus a Jew named Apollos, a native of Alexandria. He was an eloquent man, well-versed in the scriptures.

²⁵He had been instructed in the Way of the Lord; and he spoke with burning enthusiasm and taught accurately the things concerning Jesus, though he knew only the baptism of John.

²⁶He began to speak boldly in the synagogue; but when Priscilla and Aquila heard him, they took him aside and explained the Way of God to him more accurately.

²⁷And when he wished to cross over to Achaia, the believers encouraged him and wrote to the disciples to welcome him. On his arrival he greatly helped those who through grace had become believers,

²⁸for he powerfully refuted the Jews in public, showing by the scriptures that the Messiah is Jesus.

C.   Titus

(from the Third-Generation Pauline Tradition)
Recollections about Apollos from a Writer
and Community

Titus 3:13

Make every effort to send Zenas the lawyer and Apollos on their way, and see that they lack nothing.

INTRODUCTION

Who Is Apollos?

Apollos is an enigmatic character in the New Testament. His name appears in only three different writings: 1 Corinthians (1:10-17; 3:1-9, 21-23; 4:1-7; 16:12), Acts of the Apostles (18:24-28), and the letter to Titus (3:13).[1] These references are brief, yet the issues surrounding Apollos' appearance raise many questions. Mystery surrounds his character and his relationship to Paul. As is evident from Paul's own Corinthian correspondence, Apollos' presence was an occasion for much upheaval and dissension within the Corinthian community established by Paul.

When I mentioned to friends that I was writing a book about Apollos, the universal reaction was either: "Who is he?" or "How can you write a book about someone for whom the New Testament gives such little information, and who never left behind a single word?" Perhaps you had the same question on your mind when you started to read this book. On one level the question is valid. But, when you understand the approach adopted by this series of books, Paul's Social Network, you will realize that it is not only possible but also essential. To understand Apollos, as with any New Testament character, you have to place him within the social and cultural context of the world of the first century. Approaching Apollos from this starting point, we discover a world very different from our own. To view the world of the first-century Mediterranean through a lens that is closer to the way the people living at that time saw their own world is a very enriching experience.

This study on Apollos aims at achieving this goal. As with the other studies in this series, this book embraces a method of interpreting the New Testament that a growing number of scholars over the past three decades have come to appreciate as significant, namely the social-scientific approach to the interpretation of the New Testament. Simply stated, this method uses all the social and cultural sciences to throw light on the world and the text of the New Testament. In particular, it embraces the use of social and cultural sciences, such as cultural anthropology, social psychology, philosophy, and so forth. This is an essential approach for fully understanding the New Testament and the characters that populate its pages.

John H. Elliott has defined the social-scientific methodology this way:

> Social-scientific criticism of the Bible is that phase of the exegetical task which analyzes the social and cultural dimensions of the text and of its environmental context through the utilization of the perspectives, theory, models, and research of the social sciences.[2]

The use of models, as noted by Elliott, is essential to this investigation. A model can be defined as "a standard or example for imitation or comparison . . . a representation, generally in miniature, to show the construction or appearance of something."[3] Models are constructed from the social and cultural sciences, especially psychology, with the purpose of providing a wider picture within which one can understand the behavior of the people of the New Testament world. Two aspects are essential in this study: the construction of a model from the social and cultural sciences and the application of this model to the world of the first-century Mediterranean, in particular to the person of Apollos.

Only in the last few years, have I come to appreciate the value and importance of this approach for studying the New Testament. Completing this study on Apollos has convinced me even more. I hope that you, the reader, will have a similar experience.

By adopting this method, my aim is to gain an insight and understanding of Apollos as a first-century Mediterranean person. Only then will the following question be posed: given the above examination, what are the relationships between Apollos and Paul and Paul's social network? By using the applicable social and cultural sciences, this study will pay attention to four main aspects relating to Apollos: his collectivistic nature as a person of the first-century Mediterranean[4]; his relationship to Corinth and its emerging conflicts; his roots in the city of Alexandria and its contributions to his personality and identity; and, finally, his relationship to Paul and his social network.

In looking specifically at those documents that contain references to Apollos in the New Testament, two time periods must be kept in mind. The first letter to the Corinthians is a writing sent from Paul and Sosthenes to Corinth in the late fifties of the first century. In this letter, Paul gives authentic information about a contemporary of his, Apollos. The Acts of the Apostles, on the other hand, is a document from a third-generation Pauline group coming from the nineties of the first century.[5] Luke looks back on Paul's activity and his social network and gives recollections of the heroes of the faith, namely Paul and those connected with his social network. Recollections about Apollos were included to fill out the picture provided by Paul's authentic information.

Chapter 1, "Apollos: 'Sense of the Self,'" aims at understanding the person of Apollos against the cultural and social framework of the first century. By using models constructed from cultural and social psychology, we endeavor to show how an understanding of his identity, personality, and concept of self differs from a person of the twenty-first century.

Chapter 2, "Apollos: Embedded in a Collectivistic Culture," focuses on the distinction between individualistic and collectivistic cultures. Societies of the first century were collectivistic. Individuals in those cultures were concerned with belonging to a group. Their identity was always part of the group identity and their worth depended on how they were viewed in the eyes of the group. This is very different from twenty-first-century individualistic Western cultures where an individual's worth relates to his or her own success, independently of the group. This study will demonstrate how a collectivistic culture will characterize Apollos as a collectivistic self.

Chapter 3, "Apollos and Corinth: First-Generation Testimony," examines the biblical references to the situation at Corinth from a social-scientific framework. A study of conflict from a cultural and psychological perspective is of central importance. An examination of divisions, groups, and "ingroups" gives clarity to Apollos' relationships to Paul and to the Jesus group of Corinth.

Chapter 4, "Apollos and Alexandria: Third-Generation Recollections," endeavors to show how the reminiscences of Luke in the Acts of the Apostles contribute to a clearer idea of Apollos' identity. Remembered as someone at home culturally within the world of Alexandria and its Israelite community, Apollos was rooted in both cultures. Both influenced his identity. As a member of the house of Israel living outside Israel, he was grounded in his Israelite religion and was familiar with the Israelite Scriptures through their Greek translation, the Septuagint. His religion and identity were forged and strengthened through gatherings in meeting places. We have first-century archaeological evidence for such a meeting place, which was called a *proseuchē*. As the cultural center of the Hellenistic world, Alexandria must have exercised an important influence over Apollos. The questions this chapter investigates are: How does a social and cultural understanding of Hellenized Israelites contribute to a better understanding of the person of Apollos? What does an examination of Apollos' education against the background of the world of Alexandria and the thought of other well-known

Alexandrian scholars, such as Philo, contribute toward understanding his identity?

In the conclusion, "Apollos: Partner of Paul," we bring together what has emerged from the above investigations. We examine how the dynamics of small group development apply to the Jesus group of Corinth and its development. In particular, we define Apollos' relationship to Paul's social network based on this study by answering the question, is he a rival of Paul or a partner in the task of spreading the good news of the resurrected Jesus as Messiah who foreshadows the Israelite theocracy? In particular, Apollos' place within the emerging Jesus tradition will be situated more carefully.

At the end of this study, you should emerge with a deepened understanding of an important and highly educated member of Paul's social network. Such an understanding is a result not so much of acquiring intellectual knowledge but of gaining insight into a world and culture very different from today. The person of Apollos and the entire New Testament will be seen through new lenses. It will open you to new cultural experiences from which you will emerge a fuller person.

Christians believe that Jesus was God incarnate, the word become flesh. In a similar way, Christians consider the Scriptures as God's word expressed in human words, God's word become incarnate in human words. This social and cultural study of the word of the Scriptures truly makes the word incarnate—it enfleshes the word by placing it in the cultural and social human world of the first century.

Finally, I add a note regarding the use of terms such as "Jew" and "Greek" that occur in translations of the Bible. Throughout this study, I avoid the use of such terms since they are clearly anachronistic. I embrace the observations and usage of Bruce Malina and others who follow the social-science methodology regarding these terms.[6] The words "Jew" and "Judaism" are terms that rightly refer to a people and their religion that have their roots in the Babylonian Talmud, originating from the fifth century CE. It is anachronistic to use these terms to refer to the period of the New Testament or before it. The Greek words found in the New Testament are *Ioudaios* and *Ioudaismos*, which translated literally would be "Judeans (or people from Judea)" and "the way of behavior of those in Judea."

The double phrase "Judean and Greek" that Paul is accustomed to using is in fact a way of referring to two different groups of people belonging to the house of Israel in the course of the first century (see, for example, Rom 1:16; 2:9; 1 Cor 1:24). "Judean" refers to the people of the territory of Judea, while "Greek" refers to those Israelites who are civilized (as distinguished from barbarians), living in a Hellenistic way and speaking Hellenistic Greek. Simply stated, when Paul uses the designation "Judean and Greek," he is referring to those Israelites who are living in Judea and those Israelites who are living outside Israel in cities throughout the Hellenistic world.

Throughout this study we will use the designations: Judeans (or Israelites from Judea) and Hellenized Israelites to remain true to Paul's usage and that of Israelites of the first century. This will help us avoid perpetuating false notions and ideas.

The same is true of the use of the word "Christian." Today the terms Christian and Christianity are understood as referring to those who embrace a religion that has been formalized through the doctrines of the Councils of Nicea (325 CE) and Chalcedon (451 CE). In order to avoid once again every form of anachronistic thought or speech, we will refer rather to the followers of Jesus or members of a Jesus group or groups.

CHAPTER 1

Apollos: "Sense of the Self"

Social and Cultural Frameworks for Understanding a First-Century Mediterranean Person

To gain an accurate and faithful understanding of the New Testament character Apollos, it is essential to situate him within the framework of the first-century Mediterranean culture and society. In reading documents from the ancient world, we are conscious that we have to avoid all forms of anachronism. Anachronism means projecting onto the past the customs, ways of acting, and so forth that belong to a later time period, such as seeing people from the first century riding in a truck instead of on a donkey, or wearing trousers instead of flowing garments. Yet, we often fall into the trap of ignoring the ethnocentric fallacy by which we read documents of two thousand years ago with the presumption that the writers of those documents had us and our twenty-first-century experience in mind. We fail to take sufficient cognizance of the framework of the society and personages of ancient Mediterranean society that differ totally from Western society of the twenty-first century.

This opening chapter gives serious attention to the avoidance of this ethnocentric fallacy. We wish to gain an understanding in the context of the first-century Mediterranean world of Apollos' sense of self, his identity, what this sense of self meant within the context of a collectivistic (or group-oriented) culture, and how Apollos' awareness of himself was attained within a collectivistic social system.

Our procedure will be to move from the general to the particular. We will offer, first of all, an understanding of the sense of self of a first-century Mediterranean person. This understanding will act as a model that we can apply to the person of Apollos. It will also provide the foundation for our whole study in understanding Apollos as a first-century Mediterranean person. This foundation provides our starting point from which we will draw out and build up further insights about the person of Apollos.

This approach can be well illustrated through the model of the way language is used. Take two people—one from the United Kingdom, the other from the United States—as an example. They both speak English, yet we all know that their use of words can often mean very different things. If you were to show them a pair of shoes that are used for walking in the snow or for doing hard outdoor work, they would both agree that the word *boot* refers to them. Now, were you to take them outside and point to the rear end of a car, the British person would say that the word *boot* refers to it as well, while the American would disagree; for him or her it is a *trunk*. Clearly, the understanding of the word *boot* differs.

An awareness of cultural differences becomes far more important when we use words of value. What is understood as good or bad in one culture might have a different connotation in another society. This time, for example, take a first-century Mediterranean person and a twenty-first-century modern person. The first-century Mediterranean person would use the

Greek word *agathos* to identify the praiseworthy character of someone, and the American would use the English word *good* also to identify the praiseworthy character of another person. While they both identify people as *agathos/good*, this does not mean the qualities and characteristics by which they judge someone as *agathos/good* are the same. They could have a very different understanding of the meaning of *agathos/good* that arises from the context of their society.[1]

A. W. H. Adkins argues that a study of the meaning given to words, especially value-oriented words, reveals a deeper understanding of the nature of the person in the ancient Mediterranean society.[2] The usage of words, whether as terms of reference or as signifying values, must always be understood within the framework of the language of the society.

Throughout this study we will pay particular attention to the usage of words by situating them within the context of the culture, as we shall see below in Homer, who used different words in his poetry to try to express the concept of mind.

Individual, Self, Person

To gain an awareness of a first-century Mediterranean's conception of self, it will be necessary to examine the usage of words that are used to indicate this self. Before doing this, we need to be clear about what we mean when we use these terms "individual," "self," and "person."

Although individual, self, and person are used interchangeably at times, they do have distinctive reference points. Grace Gredys Harris[3] has provided an excellent analysis and definition that captures the intended reference of each of these terms. She distinguishes between them in this way: An individual is a biologistic way of conceptualizing human beings. As such, an individual is conceived as a member of the human race, a living entity alongside many other such entities. The self is a psychologistic way of conceptualization. The self is the "locus of human experience" whereby selves are seen as human beings who are centers of their own being and experience. Finally, a person is a sociologistic conceptualization whereby the human being is seen as an agent who functions as a member of a society.[4]

Terms Illustrating Individual, Self, Person

	Mode of Conceptualization	Definition	Mediterranean Society (First century)	Western Society (Twenty-first century)
Individual	biologistic	member of the human race	stress on the group/collective	stress on the individual
Self	psychologistic	"locus of human experience"	exterior experience	interior influences
Person	sociologistic	agent functioning as member of society	conformity of agent to the group actions	freedom of expression and choices of individual

While these three terms might be found in all cultures, the emphasis given to each differs within the framework of each culture.

- *Individual* (as a member of a group): In the Western world the stress rests on the individual with rights and duties. In the period of the first-century Mediterranean, the focus was rather on the group/collectivity where the individual was valued only as part of that group/collectivity.

- *Self* (the "locus of human experience"): In the Western world the importance lies on interior self-reflection that gives identity to the individual as distinct from others. Such importance is placed on respecting every individual's integrity, enabling them to give expression to their own thoughts, feelings, and opinions. In a first-century society, the focus rested on the group/collectivity that influenced the thought, feelings, and opinions of the individual. The self conformed to the thought, feelings, and opinions of the group/collectivity.

- *Person*: In the Western world a person is seen as an agent within society. Stress is placed on the individual actions of the person whose choices are carried out according to the freedom that the Western world values above all other values. In the collectivistic society of the first-century Mediterranean, the stress remained on the conformity of the person as an agent to the way of acting of all the members of a given family or group.

Society is largely determined and influenced by whether the individual or the group/collectivity is the dominant entity of influence. Attention will be given to these two poles of gravity within a society (individual or group), distinctions that are at the heart of what distinguishes a twenty-first-century society from a first-century Mediterranean society. Before examining these societal polarities of individual or group, the self will be examined as it is understood or functions within these two types of societies.

In an important essay, "The 'Self' as a Theoretical Concept," Rom Harré[5] examines the functioning of the concept of the self within different cultures. Studies of Eskimo societies have shown how Eskimo emotions demonstrated dependence on the other members of the group or society. As regards morality, only actions that related to the common good were judged to be good or virtuous.

Harré introduces a very significant insight when he argues that the level of the awareness of a dependence on or an independence from society is something that is learned. One way the individual learns this is by means of what Harré terms "psychological symbiosis."[6] By this phrase he indicates that where two persons are in a close interactive relationship, one of them supplies the other with the necessary "psychological attributes"[7] to be able to function effectively within society. A good example of this would be the way Henry Higgins interacts with and instructs Eliza Doolittle in George Bernard Shaw's *Pygmalion* (*My Fair Lady*).

From psychological studies on "mother-talk," Harré inferred that in these relationships the mother not only talks about what the child needs or intends, but also supplies the child's needs and intentions to enable the child to meet the psychological requirements necessary for functioning within a given society. While "psychological symbiosis" refers first and foremost to the way in which mothers supplement the psychological needs of their children, Harré shows that this practice is clearly applicable to situations where some people in society supplement the inadequate social interaction of others. The implications are significant. Societies do differ from one another. Their diversity is observed on many levels, not least of all in the way they construct their moral order, namely the conditions the society upholds for its members to follow. Conformity results in good standing, while rejection entails condemnation or punishment. This leads to the understanding that one's sense of self is dependent on the role to which one has been made psychologically competent through the various processes of psychological symbiosis. In Western societies, people have been given a sense of the self that stresses interiority and an inwardness that produces an awareness of oneself as an entity that reflects on itself as a psychological unity, "an inner being" that is an organizing principle of experience.

Understanding the self as the organizing unity of our fields of consciousness, as Harré describes, is specific to the Western world. Those who have developed within this world learned this understanding of the self through psychological symbiosis. The understanding of the self observed in other cultures is different from that in the Western world because of the differences within their moral order and the psychological symbiosis members of that society embraced in their development in order to function competently within that society. Harré eloquently summarizes his argument in this way:

I have proposed the explanatory hypothesis that one's sense of self is modeled on one's role as a person in this or that society, a role realized in all sorts of language-games. To think of oneself as an atomic individual, all of whose attributes are properties of an inner entity, is as culturally specific as it is to think of oneself, as some Africans do, as the spokesperson for a real collective of beings, some ancient and some yet to be manifested in bodily form, each of whom is itself but a nexus in that very network.[8]

This culturally determined understanding of the self is an important foundation on which to develop an understanding of the concept of the self within the framework of first-century Mediterranean societies. The starting point to begin investigating their sense of the self is through the usage of their language, as Adkins indicated.

The Self in the Moral Order of the First-Century Mediterranean World

Through Alexander the Great's conquests in the fourth century BCE and Rome's appropriation of those territories from the second century BCE onward, Greek culture permeated every society of the Mediterranean, producing a unified cultural way of life. In Greek culture the earliest framework for a moral order for which there is literary evidence is that of the honor ethic. A person's value as a human being depended on the estimation of others; the value of self was seen through the eyes of others, not through one's own eyes.

This is well expressed in *The Iliad*, which opens with the struggle between Achilles and Agamemnon. Achilles' wrath (*mēnis*) has been provoked because Agamemnon had taken away his slave, Briseis.

> Rage (*mēnin*)—Goddess, sing the rage of Peleus' son Achilles,

> murderous, doomed, that cost the Achaeans countless losses,
> hurling down to the House of Death so many sturdy souls,
> great fighters' souls, but made their bodies carrion,
> feasts for the dogs and birds,
> and the will of Zeus was moving toward its end.
> Begin, Muse, when the two first broke and clashed,
> Agamemnon lord of men and brilliant Achilles.
>
> (*Iliad* 1.1-8)[9]

The quarrel between Achilles and Agamemnon is more than a quarrel over a slave girl. It is a struggle over the fundamental values of Greek society that gave meaning to life and worth to the person, namely, the virtues of *timē* and *kleos*. The usual English translation of *timē* is "honor" while that of *kleos* is "fame or glory." These are not very appropriate translations as the Greek words mean much more. *Timē* does not refer to the internalized sense of self-worth that we have of ourselves (in a modern society), irrespective of what others might think. In a warrior society, *timē* refers to the visible signs of one's honor, such as the gifts or the booty the warrior acquired in battle. For Achilles, his concubine, Briseis, demonstrates his *timē*. When Agamemnon takes her away, he is not just removing Achilles' slave girl, he is also depriving Achilles of the visible sign of his value in the eyes of his men (his honor).

Another central aspect in this culture that helps to explain further the moral order of the society is the concept of a "limited goods society."[10] From an economic perspective, this means there is only so much wealth to go around. Applying this to the concept of *timē*, we immediately see the inevitable consequence: If you acquire more *timē*, I, by definition, will acquire less. If Agamemnon takes away Achilles' slave girl, Agamemnon has acquired more *timē*, and Achilles now has less. You can see how serious the matter is for Achilles: his very worth has been diminished through Agamemnon's actions. What is of central concern here is the way in which "I" am perceived and evaluated in the eyes of others. Self-worth depends on what others think of a person, not what one thinks of oneself. The psychological symbiosis that is necessary for one to function effectively within this society is directed toward the external evaluations of others. This is very different from our twenty-first-century world where a person's worth depends on his or her self-evaluation irrespective of what others think about him or her. In the ancient world there was no form of self-reflection occurring within the individual. The focus was rather on the external appropriation of what others think of the person, in other words, *kleos* (often translated as "glory," "fame," or even "reputation").

The external value given to another was the guiding and driving force of every ancient Mediterranean society, as is evidenced in the earliest surviving literary record of Western civilization. Action and glory were central to the lives of all who lived within this framework.

This sense of self as indicated above is further seen in Homer's usage of language. Bruno Snell's[11] study shows that for Homer there was no single word that captured the meaning of "mind" or even "soul," as there was in the period after Plato, to identify the seat of all thought and feeling. The word *psychē*, for example, refers to "the force which keeps the human being alive."[12] This force deserts the human being at death and flutters down to Hades.

Not only was there no single word to capture the meaning of "mind" or "soul," there was also a fragmentation within the human being: different mental activities were seen to take place in different organs of the body. Some things happened in the heart (words that are identified with *kardia*, *ētor*, or *kēr*), others in the midriff or diaphragm (*phrenes*), while still others in the lungs (*thymos*).

Homer's fragmentation of mental abilities does not make it possible for the individual to develop or grow through his or her own power or self-control. Any such development was always attributed to the action of the gods. There was the need for the infusion of the divine into the individual for him or her to attain higher things because of the lack of unity through the fragmentation of the mental abilities of the individual. A good example of this is seen in *The Iliad* when Hector is wounded by Ajax who knocked him out with a great boulder. Zeus sends Apollo to give Hector renewed strength so that he can return to the battle (see *The Iliad*, 15.259–311).

Plato brought a new understanding of the self or soul. In *The Republic*, Plato argues that the human being's fragmentation is overcome through the subordination of the functions within the soul. Through the voice of Socrates, Plato begins by asserting the parallel between the state (or society) and the individual, and he discovers within the soul the same three impulses that he observed within the state. The three impulses of the soul of which he speaks are: (1) reason that refers to the impulse that calculates and decides; (2) desire (or appetite) that embraces the bare physical instinctive cravings and impulses; and (3) spirit (or passions) that refers to those impulses of the human soul such as tenacity, enterprise, ambition, indignation. For Plato, justice occurs, or one acts in the right way, when reason rules the impulses of desire and passion. There is an order that needs to be implemented in which reason controls desire and passion. In doing so, reason achieves harmony within the soul of the individual.[13]

For Plato, the unity of the soul is that place where all thought and feeling occur. This is different from the Homeric concept where the *psychē* is considered simply as a being's life force. Plato's approach brought unity and reason together. Reason accomplishes the unity and harmony of every being. While Plato stressed the importance of the unity of the soul through the rule of reason, his approach did not do away with the earlier Homeric notions of the importance of honor and glory, namely the warrior ethic as described above. As Charles Taylor argues,

> Plato's work should probably be seen as an important contribution to a long-developing process whereby an ethic of reason and reflection gains dominance over one of action and glory. The latter is never set aside altogether.[14]

For Plato the good life is ruled by reason. Reason does not discover the correct order within oneself. What is perceived as the correct order within is a vision of the correct cosmic order outside. In the Homeric value system of honor and glory, it was the external evaluation of oneself that gave meaning and importance to life: how "I" am perceived in the eyes of others. In the thought of Plato and those who followed him, once again the external gives meaning to the internal self. The understanding of reason and right order comes from the perception of the soul's eye of true being, of the true order of the cosmos. What is exterior gives evaluation to the interior. This view is a far cry from the interiorization of the self that is at the center of our lives as twenty-first-century Western individuals living within an individualistic culture!

Application to Apollos

We have examined at length and in depth the sense of self of those living within the moral order of the first-century Mediterranean world. Its importance cannot be overemphasized as it forms the basis and foundation for our whole study on Apollos within the framework of the first-century Mediterranean cultural and social world. This examination provides initial insights into Apollos, as embedded within this first-century Mediterranean world and its values. These insights will be developed in depth in the following chapters.

Apollos' sense of self would have conformed exactly to that sense that people of the first century had. Apollos, like everyone else, was embedded in a number of groups (family, his Israelite ethnic group, his city, as well as the Jesus kinship groups). Each group contributed to Apollos' identity of self: his thoughts, feelings, and opinions derived from and conformed to those of his embedded groups. He received his identity from these groups.

Adkins' views make us aware that we can attain an insight into Apollos' sense of self by taking seriously the words of value

used in that society. His sense of worth came from acting according to the values of the group in which he was embedded. His
actions were good or bad depending on the value judgments of
his group.

Apollos' sense of self was also dependent on the role to which
he had been made psychologically competent through the pro-
cess of psychological symbiosis. He was made aware from earliest childhood that the society to which he belonged was vital to
his very existence. Their values, their thoughts, their judgments
were like a second nature to him. Apollos had been trained to
absorb these values, thoughts, and judgments as his own just as
you unconsciously absorb the air you breathe. His sense of his
own being or self-worth would have depended on the way others viewed him insofar as his actions reflected the values of the
society.

Of central importance for Apollos as a person of the first-
century Mediterranean world would have been the values of
honor and glory. In a limited goods society whatever honor
Apollos attained meant that there would have been less honor
for others. This perspective is essential for understanding the
disputes within Corinth, as we shall see in chapter 3. Within the
Jesus group in Corinth some members claimed a commitment
to Apollos ("I belong to Apollos" [1 Cor 1:12]). Because Apollos
is held up as someone to whom allegiance is owed, this would
have taken away from the glory rightfully due others. For Paul
this had serious implications. The Jesus group of Corinth belonged to Jesus Christ and through Jesus to God. To claim that
one belonged to Apollos or to Paul implied that the honor due
to Jesus and to God was lessened.

Not only would the honor/glory ethic of the warrior have
influenced his mode of thinking, reason would likewise have
influenced his thought and interpretation of the Scriptures. The
model presented above of the understanding of the soul/self
within the context of Platonic thought and its traditions also
serves to identify Apollos more fully. Apollos did not experience
a radical self-reflexivity, as we do today. Reason for Apollos was

influenced not by self-discovery, as it is for us today. Instead, reason discovered direction from outside of itself.

The foregoing discussion of the concept of the self as it emerges in the warrior ethic of the Homeric epics as well as the contrasting image of the self as portrayed by the dialogues of Plato are valuable models to use in order to understand the personality of Apollos as he emerges from the pages of the New Testament. While we have no words attributed to him in the New Testament, we do have a simple yet informative statement about him, "Now there came to Ephesus a Jew named Apollos, a native of Alexandria. He was an eloquent man, well-versed in the scriptures" (Acts 18:24).

We will discuss below the implications of Apollos' Alexandrian background as indicated in Acts 18:24 (see chap. 4). What is clear in the light of the above is the influence of Platonic thought in Alexandria. For example, from the numerous writings of Philo of Alexandria, an Israelite philosopher/theologian of the first century, we have evidence of the importance that Plato's world of ideas played on his mode of thinking. In fact, Philo interpreted the Israelite Scriptures according to this Platonic philosophical way of understanding reality. Given this evidence, it is also highly probable that Apollos' background and education had brought him into contact not only with Platonic thought, but also with Philo's approach to the interpretation of the Scriptures.

In sum, our survey of the moral order of the first-century Mediterranean world has given us our starting point. Apollos is understood by taking seriously his sense of self, which is determined by making his own the values, thoughts, and judgments of the groups in which he was embedded. Perhaps the best description of the way ancient persons, and in this instance Apollos, thought is to characterize it as "thinking socially, not psychologically."[15]

CHAPTER 2

Apollos:
Embedded in a Collectivistic
Culture

I n the previous chapter, we discussed Apollos' sense of self
as a first-century Mediterranean person. In this chapter, I
wish to develop the examination further. To understand
Apollos, as well as all who populate the pages of the New Testament, we must view them, not as individuals, but as collectivists. Since first-century Mediterranean societies were collectivistic,
we need to investigate the relationship between the individual
and the community within the framework of that society. This
leads to an important question: what does it mean to call Apollos
"a collectivist self"? Since the basic aspects of individualism and
collectivism are fairly well known today, I shall limit our examination to those aspects that will help us understand Apollos
more fully. Again, I shall discuss a model as it emerges from
studies on cultural and social psychology[1] and draw out its implications for our understanding of Apollos.

Attributes of Individualistic
and Collectivistic Cultures

Harry C. Triandis, a scholar of social and cultural psychology, defines culture in this way:

> Culture is a set of human-made objective and subjective elements that in the past have increased the probability of survival and resulted in satisfactions for the participants in an ecological niche, and thus became shared among those who could communicate with each other because they had a common language and they lived in the same time and place.[2]

There is an intrinsic link between culture and behavior. Culture is that treasure a society values as it remembers and uses what has worked in the past. New members born into a society are taught either directly or indirectly those things that have worked and are essential for survival within that society.

The connection between culture and behavior has been sketched by Triandis in this way:

> ecology → culture → socialization → personality → behavior[3]

Ecology draws attention to the geographical environment and climate that produces the means available to make life productive. The wildlife, the vegetation, the availability of water, all contribute positively or negatively to a people's way of life. An abundance of water will lead to people adopting a life and occupations around water, such as fishing. A total lack of water leads people to adopt a nomadic life consciously in search of water. Memory of what has worked in the past is handed on, preserving ways of acting, values, norms, and roles within the society, thereby producing the culture of that society. As we already discussed, parents especially socialize their children into the norms and values of the society through psychological symbiosis so that they are at home within the culture.[4] The individual either accepts these norms and values or rejects them, thus defining his or her personality. Finally, these norms, attitudes, and beliefs all define one's behavior.

Social-science studies have demonstrated that cultures understand persons either in an individualistic or a collectivistic way. In an individualistic culture, the person is understood as one who has an individual consciousness of his or her own being, as demonstrated in chapter 1, is self-reflective, motivated, and gives great importance to his or her own choices and decisions over those of the group. Are you aware that English is the only language that writes the pronoun "I" with an uppercase letter while other pronouns are left in lowercase? This reflects the nature of English-speaking cultures that prize the individual over the group! In a collectivistic culture, the individual is intrinsically part of the group—the importance and concerns of the group take precedence over those of the individual.

In a society identified as individualistic, the individual's personal goals are paramount. In a society characterized as collectivistic, the group's goals are paramount while the individual's goals largely conform to the goals of the group.

The chart[26] on the following page summarizes studies done on present-day individualistic and collectivistic cultures and illustrates clearly the differences between the two cultures. Following the chart, I shall endeavor to imagine how Apollos would have illustrated these attributes in his own life.

Despite the chart being based on studies of various societies and cultures during the past century, we can still successfully use these studies to understand the world of the first-century Mediterranean. Since these cultures were collectivistic and group centered, we can apply the collectivistic attributes to the person of Apollos to situate him fully within first-century Mediterranean culture. As a collectivist, all the attributes in the right column would be characteristic of Apollos. An examination of these eleven attributes shows how the emphasis is consistently placed on the relationship to the group. Let's look at these attributes briefly to see how they would characterize the person of Apollos.

Comparison between Attributes of Individualistic versus Collectivistic Cultures

	Individualistic Culture	Collectivistic Culture
Attributions	Attributes events to individual causes	Attributes events to external causes
Emotions	Focused on themselves; last long	Focused on others; do not last
Motivation	Performance = ability × effort; performance is an individual effort	Performance = ability + effort; performance is a group effort
Cognitions	Focus on their own needs	Focus on the needs of their ingroup
Attitudes	Self-reliance; hedonism (value the good life); competition; emotional detachment from ingroups	Sociability; interdependence; family integrity; holding an opinion that differs from the ingroup is bad
Norms	Norms are seen as less important than attitudes; equality of men and women	Norms are more important than attitudes; roles of men and women are important to identify
Values	"intellectual autonomy"; "affective autonomy"	"conservation"; "harmony"[6]
Conflict resolution	Less compromising and obliging	Obliging, compromising, try to preserve the relationship
Morality	Consistency between belief/attitude and behavior; truthfulness	Concern for others, beginning with the family and leading outward; obedience to rules
Responsibility	Individual bears responsibility	The group is responsible for the wrongdoing of its own members
Personality	Autonomy: creative, achievement-oriented	Affiliation: strong sensitivity to rejection

Attributions. In looking at the cause of events, Apollos would have ascribed them to external causes. For example, if Apollos was unable to sail for Corinth, he would have viewed it as God's will that he should not go there. An individualist would look for internal reasons that prevented him going, such as his own lack of organization to prepare for the trip in time.

Emotions. As a collectivist, Apollos' identity would have been defined by his relationship to the group in which he was embedded. His emotions would have been connected to the group and would have depended on "the other," namely the members of the group. When members of the group experienced sadness, Apollos would have identified with their sadness. He would have been sad as long as they were sad. Studies on collectivistic societies show that collectivists experience sadness more frequently than happiness.[7] Individualists, on the other hand, focus on themselves, on their own emotions, which tend to last much longer than those of collectivists.

Cognitions. This concerns what collectivists or individuals think about and how they are influenced by their thoughts. For Apollos, his thoughts would most often have been directed toward the needs of the group in which he was embedded. For example, when he was in Corinth, he would have focused on the needs of the Jesus group in Corinth and how he could respond to them. An individualist would have been more aware of and concerned about his own needs and rights. As a well-educated person from the Hellenistic world, we can imagine that Apollos must have attended the performance of many plays. Were he to see and hear, for example, the performance of *The Iliad*, he would have been really moved by the speeches of Hector and his wife Andromache when they foresee the destruction of Troy and what will happen to them after its destruction. The emotions of collectivists, like Apollos, are more easily moved than those of individualists by the presentation of such imaginary scenes.

Motivation. Regarding achievement motivation, Apollos would have been oriented toward the ingroup and the society at large. What this meant for Apollos as a collectivist was that he would have been motivated to achieve, not as an individual, but together with others. We can see this clearly in his accomplishments. Apollos' performance would never have been judged in an individualistic way as though it were a personal quality. Performance was always the outcome of a group effort. As with any group task, some persons would have expended more effort on the task, others would have made up for their effort with their abilities. By combining effort and abilities (of the members of the group) one would judge the performance (where performance = effort + ability). Apollos' role within such ingroups in Corinth would have been to motivate the group to combine their efforts and abilities.

Attitudes. Apollos' attitudes would have reflected his sociability in that he would have enjoyed living in close proximity to others. We see this in his move from Alexandria to Ephesus where the first thing he did was to seek out the Israelite "synagogue" or gathering place (Acts 18:26). His immediate reaction was to connect with his own ethnic group. When he left Ephesus, he was given a letter of recommendation to connect with the Jesus group in Corinth (Acts 18:27). In both instances, in Ephesus and in Corinth, Apollos depended on others to supply his needs. This is very different from individualists who relish in relying on their own resources to supply their needs. As a wandering preacher and a change agent, Apollos did not undertake his ministry alone. He worked in conjunction with others, relying on their help. His move to Corinth shows us that Apollos was first supported in his work of preaching by the Jesus group in Ephesus, then by the Jesus group in Corinth. Another really important attitude for Apollos would have been to ensure that his opinions conformed to the ingroup with which he was embedded—not to do so would have made him a bad character in the eyes of the group. This would have happened more unconsciously than consciously. That is not to say that he would not have tried to guide or direct the group if they deviated from the views of the wider Jesus groups. We can see this constantly in the letters of Paul. His admonitions encourage the Jesus group to which he writes to conform their attitudes to his interpretation of the resurrected Jesus as Messiah in light of the Israelite Scriptures.

Norms. As a collectivist, Apollos would have conformed to the norms of the ingroup. The proper functioning of any society or group depends on adherence to the norms that guide that group or society. For example, society at large was governed by its proper order where everyone in society had their place and order. So, the roles of men and women within the society were seen as paramount. Apollos undoubtedly upheld these norms and these roles in his interaction with all the different Jesus groups. We see these norms expressed very forcefully in the Pastoral Letters as they give specific attention to the roles of men, women, children, and slaves within the Jesus group (Titus 2:3-10).

Values. Apollos' value system would have reflected the values of his ingroups, which uniformly would have stressed good social relationships, respect for tradition, ingroup harmony, and honor of parents and elders among the most important qualities. The Jesus group in Corinth broke one of the most important values by causing discord. This explains why it was the very first issue Paul addressed when he wrote his letter to them to try to restore harmony.

Conflict resolution. In an effort to resolve the Corinthian conflict, we note that Paul used language to exhort the Jesus group there to restore their relationships. For Paul, it was important to preserve harmony within the group rather than allow the relationships to disintegrate. This approach reflects the worldview of collectivists much more than that of individualists. Paul also appeals to their obligation to end these cliques and restore harmony because they "belong to Christ." Apollos undoubtedly had the same approach as Paul, namely to preserve the harmony of the group. It is also a reality that when a situation had become truly hostile, collectivists were more likely to be outspoken in an effort to oppose the breakdown and to restore the harmony. Paul's words bear this out in his letters.

Morality. Apollos' morality would have focused on a concern for others. This concern would have been directed to members of the ingroups in which he was embedded. It would have begun with his kinship group, and moved outward to his ethnic group, his fictive kinship group, and then to the *polis* of Alexandria. Another important collectivistic dimension of morality was the importance of adhering to the rules and laws that were essential for the effective functioning of the groups.

Responsibility. Regarding the wrongdoing of a member in a group, the whole group bore responsibility for what happened. This explains why Paul addressed the issue of cliques with the whole Jesus group of Corinth. They were responsible for restoring harmony within the community. Paul did not approach the issue by identifying those individuals who were the leaders in promoting these cliques. He urged the whole community to act. As Apollos was associated with Paul in this issue, we can presume that he would have approached the issue in much the same way.

Personality. As a collectivist, Apollos would have had a keen sense of belonging. His whole nature was oriented toward affiliation. For example, when he first arrived in Ephesus, he sought out the local synagogue. This shows his sense of affiliation and his desire to be part of this fictive kinship group. This sense of belonging is illustrated again when he accepts a letter of recommendation to the new Jesus group in Corinth. This letter gave him entrance to the new group and promoted again his need to belong. Collectivists were extremely sensitive to rejection.

As we have indicated, these attributes describing Apollos and his relationship to the group will help us understand better the conflict around Apollos and other apostles within the Jesus group in Corinth. We will examine this conflict in more detail in the next chapter.

As we noted at the end of the previous chapter, our modern Western world tends to consider a person *psychologically* whereas the first-century Mediterranean world looked on a person *socially*.[8] What is meant by this? To consider a person psychologically means that one is concerned with an individual's developmental growth and uniqueness insofar as his or her behavior can be explained according to the environmental influences that have tended to contribute to this growth and behavior. On the other hand, when reading the New Testament, especially the gospels, a first-time reader is struck by the almost total lack of information regarding the psychological growth or development of Jesus of Nazareth or of any of the characters in the pages of the New Testament. This shows that our concept of viewing the individual psychologically is unknown and unimportant to the world of the New Testament.

The Mediterranean world of the first century tended to view individuals only in connection to others. This is what is termed dyadism (from the Greek, meaning "a pair").[9] A dyadic personality requires interaction with another so that one can know who one is. People think of themselves in stereotypical terms that place them in relationship to a particular role or status or group. Dyadism is "an other-directed orientation."[10]

Without even having much information about Apollos, we have still gained an enormous insight into him as a collectivistic person. The attributes of a collectivistic culture certainly apply to him. As a collectivist, Apollos would have always needed to be in relationship to a group in which he was embedded. This means that we must examine Apollos' relationship to these different groups as a way of gaining a deeper insight into his character.

Apollos: Groups in which He Was Embedded

We have become familiar with the word "embedded." In the course of the U.S. invasion of Iraq, it was used to refer to journalists who were embedded with a particular unit of the U.S. military. The term simply means to be entrenched within a particular group. In the context of the ancient Mediterranean world, it means something far deeper than the idea of a journalist being connected with a specific army unit. It indicates that very strong bonds have been forged between the individual and the group.

Collectivistic people are embedded in groups. There were many groups in the ancient Mediterranean with whom a person would have been connected, rooted, or entrenched. To know a person is to know the group in which he or she is embedded. To know the group is to know as well all those who are embedded in the group. All individuals within the group share the same perspectives, visions, values, and goals. Collectivistic members embedded in a group do not sense any distinction between themselves and the group. Three dominant values provide the glue that keeps the members of the group together: loyalty, solidarity, and attachment to the group. This glue is symbolized by the concepts of "blood, birth, or fictive birth."[11]

When examining Apollos within the framework of ancient Mediterranean society, we note that there are four foundational groups in which he was embedded: the kinship group (or family), the ethnic group, the fictive kinship group, and the *polis*. We will describe each one of these groups and how Apollos was embedded within them.

Kinship Group (Family)

Instead of "family," I prefer to speak of "kinship group." "Family" immediately conjures up—anachronistically—our Western concept of a close-knit unit of father, mother, and child(ren). In first-century Mediterranean societies (and still today in some Near Eastern countries), the kinship group was foundational for the organization of the whole society. Edward T. Hall provides a good illustration of how a person is bound by a world of hidden rules guiding relationships in the kinship group in parts of the Arab world today:

> An American these days will not normally consider the revenge of the brothers as a price for seeing a woman without her family's permission, nor will it cross his mind that she might lose her life if she chooses to be intimate with him. These are not "alternatives" which occur to him as he is weighing the choice of patterns available to him. Death of the woman and revenge on the man are within the expected range of behavior in the less Europeanized parts of

the Arab world. . . . What is being guarded is not the sister's life (though she may be deeply loved) but a centrally
located institution without which the society would perish
or be radically altered. This institution is the family. In the
Middle East the family is important because families are
tied together in a functional interlocking complex. The
accompanying network (and obligations) satisfies many of
the same functions that our government satisfies. The sister
is a sacred link between families and, like the judge in our
own culture, she has to remain above reproach.[12]

This certainly reflects the same understanding in the context
of the first-century Mediterranean world. The most important
foundational social structure in the patriarchal world of the
first-century Mediterranean was the kinship group embedded
around the father as "head" (or "patriarch"), comprising father,
mother, married sons (with their wives and their children), un-
married children, slaves, servants, retainers. Within this kinship
group, an individual was related to parents and through them
to aunts, uncles, siblings, cousins. Through marriage the individual in turn became a parent with children.

Males and females were usually identified by their father, the
head of the kinship group in which they were embedded. So,
for example, we have "James son of Zebedee and his brother,
John" (Matt 4:21), and Rebekah says, "I am the daughter of
Bethuel" (Gen 24:24). However, when the woman was married,
she was embedded in the kinship group of her husband: for
example, "Joanna, the wife of Herod's steward Chuza" (Luke
8:3). From birth, males and females were socialized into the
realization that they were sons and daughters of certain fathers
and mothers whose honor (and shame) spread over them. Males
and females were also socialized into situating themselves within
their own group. They were trained to act as it was expected of
a male or a female within that group. All spheres of life were
affected by gender. Males represented the family to the outside
world: their role was to operate within the public sphere. Fe-

males represented the family to the inside: their role was confined within the private sphere.

The biblical sources provide us with no information about Apollos' immediate kinship group. Nevertheless as a collectivist from first-century Mediterranean society, we can infer much about his kinship group. For Apollos, the foundational group in which he was embedded was the kinship group of his birth. For his whole life, this kinship group would have continued to remain foundational. This kinship group socialized Apollos to the point that he would have fit into the wider society of the community to which his kinship group belonged. This education provided Apollos with the values, norms, and ways of understanding necessary to become a fruitful member of that society.

Apollos grew up within this social structure with his father as the patriarch. His mother's role was to nurture and socialize him for the collectivistic society to which they belonged. Later, his father would have taken over his socialization to prepare him for the public role that he would have played as a male. Acts refers to him as "Apollos, a native of Alexandria" (18:24). This phrase implies that his kinship group held some standing within the city of Alexandria since this was a way of indicating elite members of society.

Ethnic Group

The next significant group in which Apollos was embedded was the house of Israel (*Ioudaios* in Acts 18:24). Apollos was socialized into the traditions and customs of the people of Israel as understood and practiced among Hellenized Israelites living outside Israel. Further, as Acts (18:24) notes, he was from Alexandria, a city where probably the largest group of Israelites outside Israel had settled over the course of many centuries.

All spheres of life for Apollos would have been influenced by his identity as a Hellenized Israelite. As such, he would have believed that he was a member of the chosen people of the God of Israel, a people that had been set apart by the God of Israel:

"So Paul stood up and with a gesture began to speak: 'You Israelites, and others who fear God, listen. The God of this people Israel chose our ancestors and made the people great during their stay in the land of Egypt, and with uplifted arm he led them out of it'" (Acts 13:16-17).

He would have lived and grown up within his own ethnic group, in the Israelite quarter of the city. Greek would have been his mother tongue. Familiarity and understanding of Israel's Sacred Scriptures would have come through the use of Hellenistic Greek. The bonds that he had with other Hellenized Israelites were deep. Next in importance to his bonds of kinship with his family members were his bonds with these members of his own ethnic heritage. The distinction between "Israelite" and "non-Israelite" would have equally applied to Apollos. While the Israelite community in Alexandria was sizable, Apollos would still have perceived himself and the members of his ethnic group as a minority compared to the Greeks and the Egyptians of Hellenistic Egypt.

Fictive Kinship

Fictive kinship describes the bond created among members of a group that is analogous to the bond and relationship that exists in the normal kinship group. The values, roles, and rules that characterize the kinship group are applied by analogy to some association whose members relate to each other as fictive siblings. Fictive kinship groups such as *collegia* (clubs) and associations were to be found in the first-century Mediterranean world. They contained structures and values analogous to a kinship group: they were often organized around one central person, who was analogous to the patriarchal father of a kinship group. However this fictive father did not have the entitlements and rights of a patriarchal father. Rather he was much like a mother's brother (maternal uncle), that is a male who presided over the group, without legal sanctioning entitlements. People could leave the fictive kin group without fear of legal sanctions. All the members of the fictive kinship group related to each other as they would to siblings, referring to each other as "brother" and "sister." Fictive kinship groups were established for various reasons. The founder of the fictive group could be a teacher, the head of a trade guild, the founder of a *collegium* ("any private association of fixed membership"[13]), or of a club consisting of voluntary associations of people coming together for a common purpose.

The structure of a fictive kinship group was a basic structure for the early Jesus groups. They were referred to as "the family of faith" (Gal 6:10). In the evolving structure that developed, the leader assumed the role of the fictive father of a kinship group. For example, in the instructions given by the writer of 1 Timothy, one of the necessary qualities set forth for the choice of a new leader of the community was that he had to have shown that he could manage his own household where he was a patriarchal father with entitlements and rights. The implication was that if he was unable to run his own household, how would he be able to run the household of believers (1 Tim 3:4-5)? Next to the kinship group itself, fictive kinship groups were significant places where people chose to embed themselves since they shared the same goals and way of life.

One important relationship within fictive kinship groups was that between teacher and disciple. This relationship was akin to the relationship of a father and son. In the New Testament, a disciple is often referred to as the son of a teacher. For example, Paul considers Timothy as his son (Phil 2:22); Peter refers to Mark as "my son" (1 Pet 5:13). Disciples were also identified as the followers of a specific teacher. Paul was identified as a student of Gamaliel (Acts 22:3).

The relationship between teacher and disciple is most important in the world of pedagogy. By knowing who the teacher is, you immediately know something about the social values and norms in which the individual had been educated. For example, in the myths of the world of Greece, the centaur Chiron was the educator of Achilles, Jason, and Asclepius. This shows they had been trained in wisdom, knowledge of medicine, and also in barbarity! Aristotle was tutor to Alexander the Great.

To know that Paul was a student of Gamaliel provides a good understanding of Paul's Israelite traditions (Acts 5:34-39; 22:3). Sources provide us with much information about Gamaliel and show us his connections to his kinship group. Josephus describes Gamaliel's kinship group (and by implication Gamaliel himself) as "a very illustrious family, and of the sect of the Pharisees, who have the reputation of being unrivalled experts in their country's laws" (*Vita*, 191). Rabbinic literature identifies him as the grandson of the great Rabbi Hillel as well as the leader of the Sanhedrin. "He may thus be understood as the greatest living authority and most revered figure in all of Judaism ca. A.D. 20–50."[14]

As leader of the school of Hillel, Gamaliel's interpretation of the law showed a more lenient approach than other rabbis, such as the Rabbi Shammai. His interpretations took a pragmatic approach to the daily living of Israelite law. As a disciple of Gamaliel, Paul was embedded into Gamaliel's school and would have adopted the same insights and approach to the interpretation of the law. Perhaps, this approach prepared Paul ultimately to be more open to Jesus' Torah teachings.

"To know the teacher or mentor was to know the disciple."[15] This is highly significant for Apollos as it helps us to situate his outlook and theological views within the framework of the early Jesus groups. Acts 18:24-28 tells us that when Apollos came to Ephesus he had been instructed in the "Way of the Lord," but only in an initial way that was limited to John's baptism. Then, Apollos encountered Priscilla and Aquila who "explained the Way of God to him more accurately." In this sense, Priscilla and Aquila were Apollos' teachers or mentors. They developed Apollos' understanding and faith in the resurrected Jesus as God's appointed Messiah who would bring about the forthcoming Israelite theocracy (or kingdom of God). Knowing that Priscilla and Aquila were Apollos' instructors, we can situate Apollos within the context of Paul's social network, which reflects Paul's Jesus-group perspectives. As the Jesus groups developed, different interpretations did evolve of Jesus' proclamation in relationship to their Israelite heritage. You can see the struggle in Acts 15 where Paul's interpretation caused keen opposition from some leaders within the Jesus group in Jerusalem. Three different interpretations are evident in this chapter. One group, members of the Jesus group in Jerusalem, insisted that circumcision was necessary for Jesus-group males and that all Israelites had to embrace this rather recent Judean ritual.[16] Another group, similar to the above, was concerned with maintaining obedience to the law of Moses and those dietary laws that were central to the way of life of all Judeans. Finally, there were the Jesus groups that Paul had founded outside Judea in the Western Diaspora, and whom Paul had declared free from all these Judean practices and rituals.

Through the instruction of Priscilla and Aquila, Apollos was brought into Paul's social network. He would have been embedded in those Jesus groups that understood their freedom from Judean customs and rituals. This meant as well that Apollos would have embraced an understanding of Jesus and his relationship to the Israelite Scriptures that Paul taught. For Paul, as it would also have been for Apollos, God's agency was working through the resurrected Jesus for the forthcoming Israelite theocracy. For Apollos entering into the Jesus group meant that he was "entering the forthcoming theocracy."[17]

Through being embedded in this Jesus group in Ephesus and then later in Corinth, Apollos entered into fictive kinship with other members of the Jesus group as his brothers and sisters. Although the Acts of the Apostles tells us very little directly about Apollos, the simple statement in Acts that "Priscilla and Aquila . . . explained the Way of God to him more accurately" (Acts 18:26) enables us to situate Apollos within the fictive kinship Jesus groups Paul had established.

The Polis

The *polis*, Apollos' city of origin, was another significant area of embeddedness for him. He is introduced in the Acts of the Apostles as "a [Judean] . . . a native of Alexandria" (Acts 18:24).

This was the widest group into which Apollos was embedded. Coming from a city, Apollos had an importance in the social and cultural context of the Roman Empire that would have far exceeded anyone from the countryside. After Rome, Alexandria was the most significant city of the Mediterranean.

We can understand how the Jesus group of Corinth would have been impressed by Apollos' origin when he came to them. In the minds of some of the Jesus group members of Corinth, Apollos' status would have exceeded that of Paul from Tarsus. In itself, the city of Tarsus was not unimportant, but it was nothing like the picture Alexandria would have evoked in the minds of first-century hearers. The image of Apollos' own background and education in the city of Alexandria would have given the Corinthians further support in their search for wisdom. In this way, Apollos' stature would have grown among some members of the Jesus group of Corinth when compared to Paul who deliberately tells the Corinthians, "When I came to you, brothers and sisters, I did not come proclaiming the mystery of God to you in lofty words or wisdom. For I decided to know nothing among you except Jesus Christ, and him crucified" (1 Cor 2:1-2). To indicate Apollos' embeddedness in the city of Alexandria explains much about Apollos and the way in which he was received by some in the Jesus group of Corinth.

In summary, within a collectivistic society, people receive their identity from the groups in which they are embedded. By taking seriously what it means to be a collectivist, we have gained insight into Apollos as a person belonging to the first-century Mediterranean culture. Through a study of the four social groups in which Apollos was embedded (his kinship, his ethnicity, his fictive kinship, and his *polis*) we gained insight into his identity and personality. These four groups could be viewed as spiraling downward from the smallest group to the widest. As an Israelite from the Western colonies, his line of vision was set on the Western Mediterranean. Through his instruction by Priscilla and Aquila, Apollos had come into contact with Paul's social network. He became part of this network through his association with these Pauline Jesus groups especially in Ephesus and Corinth. In particular, his embeddedness in Alexandria added to his stature in the eyes of many within these Jesus groups.

Apollos' Embedded Values

I wish to develop further two attributes of the collectivistic culture of first-century Mediterranean persons, namely morality and values. An understanding of these attitudes of morality and the values of faithfulness and obedience is specifically significant in understanding Apollos.

Morality

In a collectivistic culture morality derived from the values of the group, values that were essential for the group's proper functioning. A person who was socialized into the group was made aware of the importance of the way others perceived and judged one. Apollos' education, as we mentioned before, like every collectivist in the first-century Mediterranean, socialized him for life in the *polis*. Apollos' actions, his assessment of himself, were determined by the way in which he was viewed in the eyes of others. The concept of conscience that we have today in the Western world of an inner voice guiding and directing us according to what is right or wrong was unknown to the world of the first-century Mediterranean. Conscience (in Greek *syneidēsis*, "to know with" or "to think with") means etymologically that one thinks with the views of others. For an embedded individual like Apollos, conscience was the awareness of the judgments and views that others made and held with regard to morality. Conscience guided him so that he knew what others thought. The judgment and opinions of others in his ingroup were judged as very significant.

The New Testament letters instruct believers in the morality of the group. While the instructions might appear to be addressed to individuals, they are for individuals embedded in a group. They are called to listen to the voice of the group.

Apollos' moral compass was developed in the context of those groups in which he was embedded. As I argued previously, all individuals within the first-century Mediterranean were socialized from their birth by their parents, especially their mothers, in the values that operated within the context of their group. The morality that Apollos absorbed from birth and through education was the morality of the groups in which he was embedded.

First and foremost, Apollos would have been socialized in the moral values of the Israelite Scriptures as understood in the first century. The Israelite Scriptures would have formed the foundation for his moral outlook as it did for most members of the house of Israel. Further, Apollos "had been instructed in the Way of the Lord," (Acts 18:25). One needs to inquire what aspects would have been central for Apollos' own journey as well as for the instruction that he provided to others. We shall draw attention to two groups of values that are vital for the effective functioning of every Jesus group.

Faithfulness and Loyalty

A central value for every member of a group within a collectivistic world is that of *pistis* commonly translated as "faith" in the sense of devotedness to a central, significant person. For every member of a collectivistic society, *pistis* bears a much wider and deeper significance, not just in the religious sense, but in the context of the very social nature of society itself. A better translation of the word *pistis* that would capture the full range and depth of its meaning would be "faithfulness." This faithfulness can be seen on two levels:

On the objective level, it refers to "the state of being someone in whom confidence can be placed."[18] In the context of a group, this faithfulness would apply to the leader or head of the group, such as the father in a kinship group, or a leader in a fictive kinship group. This position would empower that person with the virtue of faithfulness. In a religious sense, it applies to the faithfulness of God especially to the promises God has made.

On the subjective level, faithfulness would apply to "a state of believing on the basis of the reliability of the one trusted, trust, confidence, faith in the active sense."[19] This faithfulness is expressed in trust—in loyalty—in the head or leader of the embedded group. This loyalty also extends beyond the head or leader of the group to all members of the group itself. As we would expect, in a collectivistic world, loyalty to the group and its members takes precedence over one's individual concerns and needs. Josephus offers a very poignant example of how the interest of the group takes precedence over those of the individual within the group:

> At these sacrifices prayers for the welfare of the community must take precedence over those for ourselves; for we are born for fellowship, and he who sets its claims above his private interests is specially acceptable to God. (*Against Apion*, 2.196)

This concern for the needs of the group and its members permeates the pages of the ethical instruction of the New Testament. The Golden Rule has as its foundation concern for the treatment of others: "In everything do to others as you would have them do to you; for this is the law and the prophets" (Matt 7:12). Matthew's Jesus provides instructions on concern for the other member who does not conform to the values of the group:

> If another member of the church sins against you, go and point out the fault when the two of you are alone. If the member listens to you, you have regained that one. But if you are not listened to, take one or two others along with you, so that every word may be confirmed by the evidence of two or three witnesses. If the member refuses to listen to them, tell it to the church; and if the offender refuses to listen even to the church, let such a one be to you as a Gentile and a tax collector. (Matt 18:15-17)

Let us apply these reflections now to the person of Apollos. Although he was embedded in his own kinship group, that group also formed part of a wider network of groups to which he also owed faithfulness and loyalty. Sometimes, the interests of the wider group, such as the *polis*, were different from the interests of the smaller group, the kinship group. In a collectivistic world, the resolution is very simple: the interests of the wider group take precedence over the interests of the smaller group.

In his first letter to the Corinthians, Paul gives detailed attention to these cliques and their implications. The struggle between the different cliques claiming faithfulness or loyalty to Paul, or Apollos, or Cephas (Peter) was set to divide the very unity of their faithfulness and loyalty to Christ. Paul reminds all of them that their faithfulness and loyalty to Christ is paramount. When the demands of faithfulness and loyalty collide as they obviously do in Corinth, it is loyalty to Christ and to the whole Jesus group that takes precedence. Paul's concern in addressing this issue first of all to the Corinthians lies not in the fact that cliques had arisen. Instead, it is the question of loyalty and faithfulness that is being compromised. To pursue one's own interests or the interests of the smaller group is, in effect, selfishness. As Paul says to them: "Now I appeal to you, brothers and sisters, by the name of our Lord Jesus Christ, that all of you be in agreement and that there be no divisions among you, but that you be united in the same mind and the same purpose" (1 Cor 1:10). Paul begins his appeal by invoking "the name of our Lord Jesus Christ." Jesus is the head of this fictive kinship group. To him faithfulness and loyalty are demanded. Paul also reminds his hearers that they are "brothers and sisters," using the Greek word *adelphoi*, which identifies their bond among each other as fictive brothers (and sisters). Finally, Paul asks them all to have "the same mind and the same purpose." This is what is at the heart of every collectivistic group—to be united in spirit and in purpose.

The dissensions caused by these cliques within the Jesus group provided a wonderful teaching moment for the early Jesus group of Corinth to realize that God's agents—Apollos, Paul, Cephas—were exactly this: God's instruments. They were never to replace the position that the resurrected Jesus was to hold within the context of their Jesus group. Total faithfulness and loyalty was to be given to Jesus Christ (1 Cor 1:10-17).

Being: Endurance and Obedience[20]

A further set of values that were important for those embedded within a collectivistic culture stems from their whole approach to life, to the dominant value of *being*. Every person looked on his or her position within the culture as one that was given, not chosen. The whole approach to life was to accept passively what came one's way because there was nothing that one could do to change things.

This can be illustrated by contrasting the way someone from our Western world approaches a problem or crisis with the way Apollos, a group-oriented person, would have faced a similar problem. In our modern Western world, the first thing an individual would ask is, "What can I do about it?" Action is required so that the modern person can strive to take control of the situation and hence resolve it. In Apollos' collectivistic world, that question did not arise. The worldview into which Apollos had been socialized was one that viewed his place in the world as determined and controlled by outside forces or agencies. Apollos would have approached the crisis in a passive way: he would have accepted this situation as coming from divine providence. The values that are embraced in such a worldview are ones that support the fundamental value of being, namely, endurance and obedience. This is very evident in the Letter of James:

> Be patient, therefore, beloved, until the coming of the Lord. The farmer waits for the precious crop from the earth, being patient with it until it receives the early and the late rains. You also must be patient. Strengthen your hearts, for the coming of the Lord is near. Beloved, do not grumble against one another, so that you may not be judged. See, the Judge is standing at the doors! As an example of suffering and patience, beloved, take the prophets who spoke in the name of the Lord. Indeed we call blessed those who showed

endurance. You have heard of the endurance of Job, and
you have seen the purpose of the Lord, how the Lord is
compassionate and merciful. (Jas 5:7-11)

Obedience is a hallmark virtue within the fictive kinship group
of believers. We see this again exemplified in the life of Apollos.
Obedience was owed first of all to God, that is the God of Israel.
When Apollos is introduced in the Acts of the Apostles, the writer,
Luke, says that "He had been instructed in the Way of the Lord."
Then one verse later Luke again emphasizes how Priscilla and
Aquila had further instructed him in "the Way of God" (Acts
18:25-26). Apollos' activity and way of life centered around car-
rying out the way the God of Israel had set forth. Apollos saw
his life set to carry out God's will. In the context of Apollos' life,
obedience took on a very specific nature as obedience to God.
When Priscilla and Aquila instructed Apollos further in "the Way
of God," this instruction conformed to Paul's insight into the
activity of the God of Israel in the resurrected Jesus.

Jesus himself had set the example through his obedience to
the will of his Father: "And being found in human form, he
humbled himself and became obedient to the point of death—
even death on a cross" (Phil 2:7-8). Paul presents Jesus' action
of obedience to the Father's will as the example that everyone
who is embedded within the fictive kinship group of believers
should follow: "Let the same mind be in you that was in Christ
Jesus" (Phil 2:5). Paul imitated Jesus' obedience. For Paul, obedience to God's will and grace dominated and directed his entire
life and ministry. His obedience came from his Damascus experience when the resurrected Jesus called him to be an apostle
among the nations: "Paul, called to be an apostle of Christ Jesus
by the will of God" (1 Cor 1:1); "Paul, an apostle of Christ
Jesus by the will of God" (2 Cor 1:1).

Paul calls believers to imitate this obedience of Jesus as well
as his own obedience to the will and call of God. He challenges
all believers to discern what that will of God entails for each of
them: "but be transformed by the renewing of your minds, so

that you may discern what is the will of God—what is good and acceptable and perfect" (Rom 12:2). "Finally, brothers and sisters, we ask and urge you in the Lord Jesus that, as you learned from us how you ought to live and to please God (as, in fact, you are doing) you should do so more and more. . . . For this is the will of God, your sanctification" (1 Thess 4:1, 3).

These words of Paul, especially his reflection on having the same mind as that of Jesus, are certainly words that Apollos, as part of the Pauline network, would have sought to assimilate and express in his own life. Believers are gifted with the grace that comes from God enabling them to persevere in obedience. Paul demonstrates this in his opening greeting to the Jesus group of Rome: "Jesus Christ our Lord, through whom we have received grace and apostleship to bring about the obedience of faith among all the Gentiles for the sake of his name" (Rom 1:4-5).

Apollos' situation in Ephesus gave him an openness to accept the further instruction and education that Priscilla and Aquila offered him about "the Way of the Lord." He showed obedience to the guidance of God's grace in his life, leading him to become a change agent who spread the message of God's agency working through the resurrected Jesus to establish the Israelite theocracy. Knowing the value of the long tradition of Israel's Sacred Scriptures, Apollos learned the concrete aspects that this obedience required.

Conclusion

In this and the preceding chapter, we have presented a snapshot, as it were, of a first-century Mediterranean collectivistic person, and we have applied it in particular to Apollos. There is much more that could be said about first-century Mediterranean persons. However, I have tried to hone in on aspects that would clearly delineate a first-century Mediterranean person from that of a twenty-first-century Western person. These aspects are truly relevant to the person of Apollos who is centrally located within this first-century world.

If the picture of Apollos that emerges from the above presentation appears somewhat strange to you then I have accomplished my goal. The truth is that someone living in the first-century Mediterranean was indeed very different from us living in the twenty-first-century Western world. This awareness is vital if we are to avoid what we have mentioned before, namely the ethnocentric fallacy whereby we read the past through the lenses of our own ethnocentric world.

While the New Testament gives us so little first-century biographical information about Apollos, we have been able to gain a deeper understanding of Apollos from this study of those determinate features that define a first-century Mediterranean person. He emerges as a real, live person within that first-century world.

Seen in this light, probably the most essential feature for our understanding of Apollos is to see him as a collectivist embedded in a number of groups. He had been socialized and educated to become an effective member of this collectivistic culture. This meant, as we have seen, that his attitudes, norms, and values were all influenced by this collectivistic culture. Not only was Apollos educated and socialized to function well within his kinship group, his ethnic group, and his *polis*, Apollos was further educated and socialized by Priscilla and Aquila to function within those Jesus groups belonging to Paul's social network. His background and education as a Hellenized Israelite and native of Alexandria would have contributed greatly to the Pauline Jesus groups.

Apollos demonstrated that he also made choices and decisions in his life in response to God's initiative. He was in control of his life only to the extent that he was a Hellenized Israelite open to obedience to the God of Israel who had called him to embrace "the Way of the Lord" (Acts 18:25). He did not convert but continued to obey and subjected himself to God's will. At the same time, given the context of the collectivistic world of the first century, Apollos' life was determined by the social situations in which he found himself. He was accepted by the Jesus group in

Corinth, yet the success of his preaching in Corinth was outside his own control. Every collectivistic person works with others; Apollos' own performance was matched by the efforts and abilities of others. On the one hand, external forces used his preaching as an opportunity to separate themselves from the wider group in Corinth. On the other hand, Apollos' message was vetted by Paul, the founder of the Jesus group in Corinth. His success or failure depended on the context of the situation and group in which he found himself, and the forces operating within that context.

In the next two chapters, we will devote our examination to the New Testament information about Apollos by situating it within the social and cultural world of the first-century Mediterranean. As we noted before, two major writings speak about Apollos: 1 Corinthians and the Acts of the Apostles. We will examine these passages in their chronological order so that we will able to see the growth and development of an understanding of Apollos. In the next chapter we examine in detail Apollos' relationship to the Corinthian Jesus group, to Paul's social network, and to what further light that sheds on the person, Apollos.

CHAPTER 3

Apollos and Corinth: First-Generation Testimony

In our previous two chapters, we situated Apollos as a collectivist within the cultural and social world of the first-century Mediterranean. This study provided us with good insight into his collectivistic personality, the groups in which he was embedded, and the attitudes and values stemming from this collectivistic culture. In all this, we gained an appreciation for how remarkably different a collectivistic personality is from our modern twenty-first-century individualistic personality. In this and the following chapter, we take the inquiry further by examining what we can glean from our sources about the personality and activities of Apollos as understood against the backdrop of the cultural and social world of the first century.

Apollos did not leave behind any written text. None of his spoken words were recorded by others. To gain a deeper understanding of Apollos, we have to rely on the testimony of others. We depend on two sources for our knowledge of Apollos: Paul's first letter to the Corinthians and Luke's Acts of the Apostles. To understand this information correctly, I intend to follow the path mapped out by Bruce Malina in the inaugural volume in this series on Paul's social network.[1] In focusing on Timothy, Paul's closest associate, Malina examined the way Timothy was seen by the different generations of Paul's social network. Using this as a model, I shall examine in sequence how the different generations of Paul's social network viewed Apollos.

In this context, a generation is defined as "a single step in natural descent, as of human beings, animals, or plants."[2] In this concept of a generation, the sequence in a line of descent from a specific person is significant. In the realm of the followers of Jesus, the term generation starts with Jesus himself as the ancestor from whom descent is traced. Since our study focuses on Paul's social network, the ancestor from whom descent is determined is Paul. By adapting the chart constructed by Malina in relation to Jesus, we can outline the successive generations in relation to Paul in this way:[3]

Pauline Generations

First generation	Second generation	Third generation
Paul, Timothy, Priscilla and Aquila, *Apollos*	Writer of 2 Thessalonians Recipients of 2 Thessalonians	Luke (Luke–Acts), 1–2 Timothy, Titus, Colossians, Ephesians, Hebrews
Collection of Paul's words	2 Thessalonians	Story of Paul, Timothy and Titus *Apollos*
Greek Lord Jesus Groups	Greek Lord Jesus Groups	Greek Lord Jesus Groups
Group formation based on the coming kingdom	Jesus' celestial activity as we await the kingdom	Reformed group formation with kingdom in abeyance

The differences in the three Pauline generations are very distinct. The first Pauline generation included Paul and his close

associates such as Timothy, Silas, Barnabas, and the like. Among
these one would include Priscilla and Aquila as well as Apollos.
The writings of Paul and his coworkers contain the historical
recollections and descriptions of events that had occurred and
that prompted the actual writing of the letter. Such was the case
with Paul's first letter to the Corinthians. Paul received a letter
from the Corinthians asking him many questions and he learned
of a number of problems within the community. To answer their
questions and to respond to their problems, Paul wrote this letter. It reflects the history of the events and gives insight into
Paul's thought and actual words. This letter, then, belongs to the
first Pauline generation.

The second Pauline generation embraced the second letter to
the Thessalonians and the Thessalonian Jesus group that received this letter. Paul had died by this time. This generation's
concern was no longer with Paul and his generation, but with
new problems and issues that had arisen after his death. Their
concern was rather with Paul's message and its relevance for
their world and context.

The third Pauline generation included the Acts of the Apostles,
the Pastoral Letters, as well as the letters to the Colossians, Ephe-
sians, and Hebrews. For our purposes, Luke's Acts of the Apostles
occupies our attention. This third generation returned attention
to the person of Paul and strove to collect the memories related
to Paul and his associates. These recollections are central to the
narrative of the Acts of the Apostles. Malina refers to this as "the
principle of third-generation interest."[4] The interest of this third
generation was with the details of Paul's story and his social
network. Half of the Acts of the Apostles is devoted to Luke's
story of Paul and the network of those involved with him. It is
in this context that Apollos appears. Much of what we did not
know in the first-generation record of Paul's letters is fleshed out
in this third-generation document, the Acts of the Apostles.

As we indicated above, our information about Paul's social
network is derived from the first and third generations. This
present chapter focuses on authentic information gleaned from

this first-generation source, Paul's first letter to the Corinthians. From this letter, we gain insight into the Jesus group of Corinth that was founded by Paul, the person of Apollos, and his relationship to Paul's social network. (The next chapter will focus on the recollections presented in the third Pauline generation text by Luke, the Acts of the Apostles.)

An Agonistic Culture

Conflict within the Jesus Group of Corinth

The foundation for our reflections on the personality and activities of Apollos stems from the opening chapters of Paul's first letter to the Corinthians. Paul mentions Apollos in five passages in this letter (1 Cor 1:10-17; 3:1-9, 21-23; 4:1-7; and 16:12). They speak about cliques that had formed around Paul, Apollos, and Cephas. The formation of a clique in the name of Apollos points to the high regard that this Jesus group of Corinth held for Apollos. These passages also point to a relationship between Apollos and Paul. We will examine these passages in 1 Corinthians by focusing on Apollos' embeddedness within this Jesus group of Corinth and the social relations that arose from this embeddedness. A deeper understanding of the person of Apollos emerges from Paul's testimony as we read it within the framework of his social and cultural world.

A Culture Prone to Conflict

The Mediterranean culture of the first century has been identified as an agonistic culture. The word agonistic is derived from the Greek word *agōn*, which indicates a contest, struggle, or a fight. Originally, the word referred to an athletic contest, but over time it referred to any contest between equal parties. In New Testament writings, it was used in a moral or spiritual sense, as in Hebrews 12:1, "let us run with perseverance the race [literally the contests (*agōna*)] that is set before us."[5]

The Mediterranean culture of the first century was indeed agonistic. This culture was prone to conflict as the gospels and the Acts of the Apostles demonstrate. Frequently, Jesus and the apostles were engaged in disputes, controversies, and conflicts. Jesus' life culminated in arrest, trial, and ultimately death. In general, the conflict revolved around the core societal values of honor and shame. As we have already noted in chapter 1 of this study, honor (and consequent glory) referred to the way one was considered or viewed in the eyes of the community; it was, as Malina and Pilch refer to it, "public recognition."[6]

Jesus posed a challenge to the honor of the Judean leaders and the Roman authorities. Both groups saw Jesus undermining their positions within society. Their honor in the eyes of the community was threatened. The same was true of the apostles in the Acts of the Apostles.

Every person in society was judged to be honorable and that honor was fiercely guarded and protected. People entered into conflict with others, especially their equals, as a way of undermining the other's honor and of increasing their own honor. John Pilch refers to this as a "cultural game"; through "challenge and response" individuals strove to catch their adversary off-guard.[7] "Challenge and response" constituted an agonistic method of interaction in the Mediterranean culture of the first century. The culture comprised constant conflict in which social equals strove for one-upmanship. The winner acquired honor, the loser shame. The action began with an initial challenge intended to undermine another's honor. The latter had to respond to this challenge while at the same time issuing another challenge. So the stakes were raised higher!

The hope was that the adversary would not be able to respond appropriately. As a result, their own honor would have been increased. In a limited goods society, as noted in chapter 1, if one person acquired something more, of necessity the other must have had less. In a similar way, if one person gained more honor through challenges or disputes, the other person would have had less honor.

A good analogy occurs in our modern world where our political environment is clearly agonistic. Here, one candidate vies with another for a particular position. Campaigns are conducted through "challenge and response." The successful candidate increases his or her honor at the expense of the other candidate who appears not to meet this challenge. The latter ends up with less honor in the eyes of the community.

Cliques among the Jesus Group of Corinth

Malina and Pilch note that "for Mediterranean anthropologists, the second most important social institution after the family or kin group in this culture area is the coalition."[8] We did not choose our family. We were born into it. In contrast, a coalition is a free association group that we enter for a limited period of time to accomplish a certain purpose. Among the many different types of coalitions, one that is of interest to us in this particular context is the clique. We define a clique as an exclusive group of people with a specific identity within a larger group who have come together to meet their common interests and needs.

The English word "clique" is derived from the French verb *cliquer*, which means "to make a noise."[9] It is an onomatopoeia; its very sound captures its meaning. The etymology embraces the idea of an exclusive group of people within a larger group who make their associated presence clearly known! They identify and associate more with one another than with the whole group. People embedded in cliques compare themselves to others and give themselves a sense of superiority.

While the terms cliques and factions tend to be used today almost interchangeably, it is important to distinguish them in a number of ways. A faction, as distinguished from a clique, is recruited by a single person with the intent of achieving a goal chosen by the single, central person. Jesus recruited a faction to assist in his goal of proclaiming the forthcoming theocracy, the kingdom of God. A clique, on the other hand, is a coalition whose members associate regularly with each other on the basis of affection and common interests, and possess a marked sense of identity. Cliques have no specific goals and are not recruited by single, central people. Hence I think it is more appropriate to call the subgroups that formed in Corinth cliques. As such, they formed with the intent of comparing themselves to others within the Jesus group of Corinth. They considered themselves better!

In a collectivistic culture, people are known by what cultural anthropologists term "their dyad," their relationship to someone or something else. By claiming "I belong to Paul," or "I belong to Apollos," the clique uses the person of Paul or Apollos to give them their dyadic identity and, more important, their honor. Both Paul and Apollos were well known and respected within the world of Corinth. Identification with either of them gave insight into those who belonged to the clique that claimed their name. The honor associated with Paul or with Apollos would have been the same honor ascribed to the members of the clique. Since honor is a public acknowledgment or opinion that all hold regarding a certain person, members of the clique would have ascribed to themselves this same honor.

Against this cultural background, the divisions within the Jesus group of Corinth become understandable. The statements, "'I belong to Paul,' or 'I belong to Apollos'" (1:12) are references made to cliques that had formed around important change agents within the context of the Jesus group of Corinth. They identified themselves with certain change agents on the basis of a bond they believed had been established between the person who was baptized and the one who performed the baptism.

They applied the language of fictive kinship to the relationship between the believer and the one who baptized. For Paul, the cliques that had developed around Apollos, Cephas (or Peter), and even himself were wrong because they divided the unity of the community of Jesus' followers. Or, to use another Pauline phrase, they had destroyed the unity of the Body of Christ. Faced with these cliques, Paul's response was to remind them of their primary embeddedness in the person of Jesus Christ (1 Cor 1:10-17). By its very nature, a clique implies a group of people within a wider group who compare themselves with others in the group and consider themselves better than they are. This runs counter to the whole nature of a Jesus group.

Paul strongly opposed these cliques because they had lost their understanding of the meaning of baptism. As a ritual, baptism brought the Israelite from the outgroup to the ingroup and ultimately into a social relationship in Christ. Through birth the Israelite was placed in a social relationship "in Israel"; through baptism the Israelite was brought into a social relationship "in Christ."[10]

Paul argues that by claiming to belong to Paul or Apollos, the Corinthians were thinking on the human level (3:4). They forgot that Paul and Apollos were simply God's servants working on behalf of God who gave the growth (3:5-6). At the conclusion to this section (3:21-23), Paul expresses the effects of baptism clearly: "So let no one boast about human leaders. For all things are yours, whether Paul or Apollos or Cephas or the world or life or death or the present or the future—all belong to you, and you belong to Christ, and Christ belongs to God." Paul did not conceive of baptism as John the Baptist did, as a forgiveness of sins and a demonstration of repentance. Instead, he understood that baptism brought one into a bond with the resurrected Jesus. In this way of thinking, everything belongs to the one baptized, and all the baptized belong to Christ, who belongs to God. Paul reversed the whole way of thinking of the Jesus group of Corinth. Instead of belonging to Paul or to Apollos, Paul and Apollos belonged to them because they belonged to Christ. This is the effect of the death of Jesus. By being brought "in Christ" through baptism, one is brought into a unique relationship to all those who are baptized.

For Paul, the Jesus group of Corinth belonged to no one but to Christ, who in turn belongs to God. The dyadic identity that was established in baptism was to Christ (and not to Paul, or Apollos, or Cephas). All cliques were brought to an end since the only person they could belong to was Christ alone.

It was perhaps inevitable that a clique would form around Apollos. Characteristically, Corinthians searched for wisdom.

Apollos, from Alexandria with his "eloquent speech," would have immediately attracted interest, an audience, and many "fans." The focus of this clique's attention turned to Apollos, which we have indicated ran counter to the nature of a Jesus group that belonged to Jesus (or to God). This clique replaced Jesus with a focus on his change agent, Apollos.

The Conflict (1 Cor 1:10–3:23)

Paul's Understanding of Jesus Messiah

To understand Apollos' connection to Corinth and the formation of a clique around his name, it is necessary first of all to outline in detail the message Paul preached, his interaction with Corinth, and the formation of a Jesus group there. This is the context into which Apollos entered when he went to Corinth.

When Saul encountered Stephen, one of the first followers of Jesus, the death of Jesus on the cross constituted the greatest difficulty for him. He could not accept Jesus as God's Messiah, as the followers of Jesus identified him. When he writes in his letter to the Galatians, "Cursed is everyone who hangs on a tree" (Gal 3:13), he is quoting the book of Deuteronomy: "[F]or anyone hung on a tree is under God's curse" (Deut 21:23). In Saul's mind, Jesus' death on the cross was a convincing sign that Jesus was under God's curse.

Paul's experience on the road to Damascus (Acts 9:1-18) changed everything. According to cross-cultural psychology, this experience is called an "alternate state of consciousness." Dreams, visions, trances, and comas are but a few of the various alternate states of consciousness that human beings experience along with the normal state of consciousness. At times, a personally significant alternate state of consciousness may result in changes that radically influence people in their thinking, feeling, sensing, and perceiving.

When Paul says, "I received it through a revelation of Jesus Christ" (Gal 1:12), he encounters another level of reality that affects his consciousness. This experience of the resurrected Jesus embraces the alternate reality of the divine through a state of consciousness that is "nonrational but not irrational."[11] Our modern world refuses to accept such alternate-state-of-consciousness experiences as valid for everyday social interaction. Yet, this is, in fact, out of step with the experiences of so many societies in the past and even today. As Pilch states:

> Cultural anthropologists have discovered that approximately 90 percent of the cultures on the face of this planet have and enjoy the ability to enter into trance, ecstasy, or a similar altered state of consciousness with ease. The percentage is highest among Native Americans, but still high among circum-Mediterranean cultures.

Pilch goes on to describe such an altered state of consciousness:

> Studies of this phenomenon indicate that it follows a pattern. The content of the experience is often vacuous; one's culture provides the information needed to interpret the experience. The people one sees are not recognized at first. Then, after an assurance from that person ("Do not be afraid") and a revelation of identity ("It is I, N.N."), the one experiencing the vision or trance can dialogue with the person seen. In general, experiences in altered states of consciousness provide the person with new information or, more commonly, solutions to troubling problems (this includes healing, as in the visions experienced at Asclepian healing shrines).[12]

Paul's conviction of the reality of this experience was just as self-evident for Paul as were his "normal" encounters with anyone, such as his coworkers. Following his alternate state of consciousness, Paul took time to make sense of his experience of the resurrected Jesus against the background of his Israelite faith. He spent three years in the Arabian Desert reflecting on this experience thorough the eyes of his Israelite sacred writings (Gal 1:17).

This alternate state of consciousness provided Paul with a conviction and a starting point: the resurrected Jesus is alive. In this event, God's agency instituted something new. Over the centuries, the Israelites had hoped that God would establish God's rule over Israel (in other words, that God would establish Israel's theocracy). Paul saw these hopes inaugurated in the resurrected Jesus. The God of Israel constituted the resurrected Jesus as Messiah to usher in this Israelite theocracy.

When the Romans conquered Judea in 63 BCE, the Israelites perceived that the Romans had brought shame to the house of Israel. Given their cultural world, they hoped that their God would liberate them from Roman rule, inaugurate God's kingdom over Israel, and restore their honor. With his experience of the resurrected Jesus, Paul understood that the beginning of the restoration of that honor had begun. The essence of Paul's message is simply stated: God's agency has begun with the resurrected Jesus constituted as Messiah who foreshadows the coming of the Israelite theocracy. The resurrected Jesus Messiah was an evident sign that the God of Israel was to restore God's kingdom, God's theocracy, and, with it, Israel's honor among the nations.

Paul's message of the inauguration of the Israelite theocracy explains why Paul's audience would have welcomed it. It would have answered the longing of all Israelites to have their honor restored. Living as a conquered people among the nations was a situation of shame. Paul's message assured them of God's agency to restore the honor of God's people through the restoration of their theocracy.

Paul as Change Agent

In proclaiming his message about the resurrected Jesus, Paul functioned as a "change agent." Bruce Malina and John Pilch define a change agent as "a person who communicates information about some innovation to some designated receiving group on behalf of some change agency."[13] In the New Testament documents, God is the agency who initiates the change. In the first generation, the apostles were seen to be change agents in that they experienced the resurrected Jesus who commissioned them on behalf of the God of Israel in their role as change agents to the Israelites. Although Paul was not among Jesus' historical followers, he was clearly constituted an apostle and a change agent. In Paul's alternate state of consciousness experience (Gal 1:1, 10-12), the resurrected Jesus commissioned Paul to go to the Israelites (Judeans and Hellenists) to announce the message that the God of Israel raised Jesus of Nazareth from the dead and appointed the resurrected Jesus as Messiah, foreshadowing the establishment of the long-awaited Israelite theocracy.

As a change agent, Paul moved throughout non-Israelite *poleis* (cities) in the northwest Mediterranean (modern Turkey and Greece), visiting minority Israelite communities and communicating an awareness of the need to change. The change envisaged by Paul was the need to accept the resurrected Jesus as God's Messiah who was about to establish the Israelite theocracy. Paul challenged these Israelite communities to lead a way of life influenced by God's agency of change begun with the resurrected Jesus. His task was to make them aware of the need to change.

Those who accepted this need to change became members of Israelite Jesus groups. In founding these new Jesus groups, Paul was never able to address all the situations and issues. Hence, the need to write letters to the Jesus groups to answer further issues that had emerged.

Apollos is also to be considered a change agent as I shall demonstrate in the next chapter when examining Luke's recollections of Apollos in the Acts of the Apostles. There Luke provides the background to Apollos coming to Corinth.

An Ingroup Conflict

The conflict within the Jesus group of Corinth has been rightly termed an "ingroup conflict." Bruce Malina and Jerome Neyrey distinguish between ingroups and outgroups, a distinction that helps us understand what is happening in the Jesus group of Corinth:

> The groups in which a person is embedded form "in-groups'"
> in comparison with other groups, "out-groups," that do not
> command a person's allegiance and commitment. In-groups
> consist of persons who share a common fate because they
> have been generally rooted in similar circumstances of birth
> and place of origin (generation and geography).[14]

The ingroup to which Paul wrote in the first letter to the Corinthians was a Hellenized Israelite Jesus group living in the midst of non-Israelites. As such, Hellenized Israelites living in Corinth belonged to a group that was held by the story of their origins from Abraham and read the same Israelite Sacred Writings in Greek. When Paul went to Corinth and proclaimed his gospel to the Hellenized Israelites there, his aim was not to convert them to another faith (that is an anachronistic twenty-first-century way of conceiving what Paul was doing). Instead, Paul's message was to convince them that God was at work in the resurrected Jesus as Messiah to create an Israelite theocracy.

As an ingroup, all the members of this Jesus group of Corinth were of the same ethnic origin. As Hellenized Israelites, they possessed the same mythological traditions that formed their identity and gave them direction for the future. These Hellenized Israelites had embraced Paul's message that the resurrected Jesus was the one spoken about in their sacred writings, God's Messiah, who would inaugurate God's kingdom. This belief bonded them together and gave them an identity. As Hellenized Israelites, they shared together the same vision and it challenged them to act in a way that was true to the belief that in the resurrected Jesus the God of Israel was about to establish the kingdom.

Paul's concern, as we shall indicate, was that the bonds that united them were beginning to tear apart. There was a simple cause for this pending rupture: they had turned their focus away from God as the agency of the change to the change agents, namely Paul or Apollos or Cephas.

Apollos in Relation to Paul and His Social Network

The body of 1 Corinthians opens with an inclusion. The same persons, Paul, Apollos, and Cephas, are placed in the same order at the beginning and the end of the first issue that Paul addresses in the letter. "What I mean is that each of you says, 'I belong to Paul,' or 'I belong to Apollos,' or 'I belong to Cephas,' or 'I belong to Christ'" (1 Cor 1:12), and "So let no one boast about human leaders. For all things are yours, whether Paul or Apollos or Cephas or the world or life or death or the present or the future— all belong to you, and you belong to Christ, and Christ belongs to God" (1 Cor 3:21-23). This inclusion establishes section 1:10–3:23 as a common unit. Attention is drawn to a common theme that runs throughout this section, namely the formation of cliques within the ingroup.

From a close reading of 1 Corinthians 1:10–3:23, we can gain insight into the relationship between Paul and Apollos. Paul does not blame Apollos for the divisions that have occurred. He goes out of his way to stress that he and Apollos are working in harmony, not in opposition to each other. They share the same aim, the proclamation of the gospel of God concerning the resurrected Jesus as God's Messiah who is inaugurating Israel's theocracy. It seems that Apollos followed Paul in Corinth, as Paul says, "I planted, Apollos watered, but God gave the growth" (1 Cor 3:6). Paul stresses that God is the agency to whom attention must be directed, "So neither the one who plants nor the one who waters is anything, but only God who gives the growth" (3:7). Paul implies further that he and Apollos are working together, "The one who plants and the one who waters have a common purpose, and each will receive wages according to the labor of each. For we are God's servants, working together; you are God's field, God's building" (3:8-9).

Paul's first association with Corinth was very different from most of the other cities where he had established Jesus groups. Most often, Paul's sojourn in a city was limited to a few weeks. He was then forced to move on because of the rejection or opposition generated against his message (see, for example, his time in Thessalonica [Acts 17:1-10] or Athens [17:16-34]). With Corinth, things were different. Perhaps, because it was a very cosmopolitan city accustomed to welcoming differing viewpoints, Paul's preaching was easily tolerated. In Corinth, Paul was the change agent who established a Jesus group there. He did not immediately move on, but remained there for eighteen months (18:11). During those eighteen months, he deepened their understanding of his proclamation and its ramifications. Without doubt they should have gotten to know Paul's teaching well!

Why did members of the Jesus group of Corinth become so caught up in rivalries and in the formation of cliques to support one or the other of the change agents? Why did this occur in Corinth when it did not happen elsewhere? The answer lies in the cultural context of the city of Corinth itself. From records about Corinth taken from ancient writers there is ample testimony showing the Corinthians getting caught up in over-zealous enthusiasm for orators who visited their city.

From the writings of Dio Chrysostom, we glean some interesting insights into the culture of oratory and the zeal for wisdom that distinguished the city of Corinth. I quote three extracts from Dio Chrysostom because they are extremely relevant and helpful in understanding the cultural forces at work within Corinth. Dio Chrysostom writes that when he came to cities of the empire such as Corinth he advised:

> If I really like foreign travel, I should, he says, visit the greatest cities escorted with much enthusiasm [*zēlos*] and éclat [*philotimia*], the recipients of my visits being grateful for my presence and begging me to address them and advise them and flocking around my doors from early dawn, all without my having incurred any expense or having made any contribution. (47.22)

Dio Chrysostom describes Corinth at the time of Diogenes in this way:

> That was the time, too, when one could hear crowds of wretched Sophists around Poseidon's temple shouting and reviling one another, and their disciples, as they were called, fighting with one another, many writers reading aloud their stupid works, many poets reciting their poems while others applauded them . . . , and peddlers not a few peddling whatever they happened to have. (8.9)

Dio Chrysostom further narrates how a disciple strove to imitate his master:

> For whoever really follows anyone surely knows what that person was like, and by imitating his acts and words he tries as best he can to make himself like him. But that is precisely, it seems, what the pupil [*ho mathētēs*] does—by imitating his teacher and paying heed to him he tries to acquire his art. (55.4-5)

The above quotations explain Paul's concern about these cliques that have formed. Their behavior is what would have been expected of those Corinthians who held in admiration wisdom speakers, Sophists, and anyone with the ability to express themselves through great rhetorical eloquence. Paul's concern was that they had lost sight of the essence of the message he proclaimed, a message that focused on the resurrected Jesus who, as God's agent, was to establish a forthcoming Israelite theocracy.

For Paul, the central issue concerned the origin of wisdom: is wisdom of human origin, or of the spirit (1 Cor 2:1-5)? Paul reminded the Corinthians of the way in which he exercised his role as a change agent among them. He did not go to them as a preacher who relied on his own abilities to convince the Corinthians of the truth of his message through lofty words of eloquence and philosophical reasoning. Instead, the change was initiated through the power of the Spirit of God working in them.

These experiences of the Spirit that transformed Israelites into Jesus-group members are referred to as those alternate states of consciousness that we discussed above. The Jesus-group experiences to which Paul refers are all attributed to the power or the gifts of the Spirit. The wisdom that the Jesus-group members received came through revelations that occurred in these alternate states of consciousness. These revelations come through the Spirit of God, and it is the same Spirit that enables the interpretation of these revelations.

At issue within the Jesus group of Corinth was wisdom. For Paul, all Jesus-group wisdom came from the Spirit of God that originates with God through Jesus Christ crucified. Contrasted to this "spiritual wisdom" was human wisdom or the wisdom of this age (2:6, 13). Paul saw that the different cliques among the Jesus group of Corinth resulted from different attractions toward wisdom.

Now, we can see where the problem lies. Paul and Apollos represented two different approaches as teachers and change agents. Paul relied upon the wisdom that came from the Spirit. Apollos, on the other hand, must have based himself on the eloquence of his speech. This deduction will be supported by what we will see in the next chapter where recollections of Apollos are preserved in the Acts of the Apostles. These recollections state that "He was an eloquent man, well-versed in the scriptures. He had been instructed in the Way of the Lord; and he spoke with burning enthusiasm" (Acts 18:24-25). That Apollos was "an eloquent man" supports the deduction that he used human wisdom in his teaching and preaching in the Jesus group of Corinth. But, Apollos did not rely on only the power of human rhetoric. Acts 18:25 indicates that he was imbued with God's Spirit ("he spoke with burning enthusiasm"). He too relied on God's Spirit in his activity as teacher or as change agent. But, differently from Paul, he seemed to use his rhetorical powers in conjunction with the power of the Spirit. Here misunderstanding occurred within the Jesus group of Corinth. They were attracted to Apollos' rhetorical wisdom and skills and focused upon these exclusively. This gave rise to the "Apollos clique" within the Jesus group of Corinth.

It is likely that Paul alludes to Apollos in his very critique of wisdom: "Where is the one who is wise [*sophos*]? Where is the scribe [*grammateus*]? Where is the debater [*suzētētēs*] of this age?" (1:20). These three words reflect the world of human wisdom. The *grammateus* is an official title directed to those holding an important public office "at Athens and elsewhere" such as a "secretary or a registrar," (literally "one who traces or marks out").[15] The word *suzētētēs* is found only here in the letter to the Corinthians. It means a "debater" related to the word *suzētēsis*, which means "a discussion in the course of which disputants persistently advocate/sponsor a particular point of view."[16] Paul consciously distanced himself from any connection to wisdom that formed the basis for preaching or teaching on Christ. For Paul, this distracted from the central message that rested on the cross and the resurrected Jesus. From this, we can deduce that it is likely that Apollos' preaching and teaching were stamped with a Hellenistic wisdom dimension. Some in the Jesus group of Corinth certainly picked up on this Hellenistic wisdom perspective and appropriated it in their own way. This would have led to a stress on and insight into Hellenistic wisdom speculation with which Paul would not have been comfortable. Paul felt it necessary to set forth very clearly his own concerns and perspective.

Apollos never intended to cause divisions within the Corinthian community. Nevertheless, the unintended consequence of his eloquent wisdom-based preaching and teaching did result in divisions within the community Paul had established. From what Paul says about Apollos, it is clear that he does not demonstrate any animosity against Apollos. The difficulties are rather with the Jesus group of Corinth itself. On several occasions in this letter, Paul goes out of his way to stress that he and Apollos are working together. "I planted, Apollos watered, but God gave the growth" (3:6). "For we are God's servants, working together" (3:9).

At the end of the first letter to the Corinthians, Paul notes that he had encouraged Apollos to travel to Corinth to address the problems: "Now concerning our brother Apollos, I strongly urged him to visit you with the other brothers, but he was not at all willing to come now. He will come when he has the opportunity" (16:12). The phrase "Now concerning," which opens verse 12 is a phrase that has been used throughout this letter to indicate Paul's response to matters that the Corinthian community had raised. It seems that the Corinthians must have asked Paul to send Apollos to them.[17] This text further implies that Apollos must have been working in close proximity to Paul for the two of them to be able to discuss the possibility of Apollos' return to Corinth.

While an alternate reading of this text implies that God's will prevented Apollos from returning, it makes perfect sense to see that it was Apollos' decision not to return now as the original text states: "Apollos was not at all willing to come now." This poses the natural question: why did Apollos not wish to go to Corinth at the request of the Corinthians, especially those who gave their allegiance to him? From Apollos' unwillingness Malina deduces "that Apollos did not initiate the clique named after him, since he is not willing to come to Corinth."[18] This makes perfect sense. Had Apollos been in the first place eager for a group to show allegiance to him and to follow his teachings and instructions, it would have been natural for him to want to return to them as soon as possible. Further, if Apollos was in close association with Paul, he would have been aware of the trouble that was been caused by the various cliques within the community. From Apollos' reluctance to return, it seems to me the logical conclusion that can be inferred is that Apollos feared that his very presence could make the situation more difficult instead of improving things.

Ben Witherington evaluates the situation in this way:

> If Apollos's will is in view, as seems likely, this suggests that Apollos did not want to add fuel to the fire of Corinthian party spirit and to their playing of favorites. But Paul makes it clear that he himself did not impede Apollos from returning. Indeed, he strongly urged it. In Paul's view, he and Apollos are not at odds but are coworkers in the same cause.[19]

Witherington's evaluation supports well my reading of the situation. Apollos' reluctance to return immediately to Corinth must point to the conclusion that he was afraid that his presence in Corinth would stir up the cliques more and lead to their continued hostility among each other. This would have damaged the very intent that Paul had for fostering unity. It is interesting to see that Paul and Apollos judge the possible return of Apollos to Corinth differently. Paul was of the opinion that Apollos' presence could help to support Paul's position and bring an end to the conflicts. Apollos, on the other hand, seems to have been fearful of further damaging an already delicate situation. Saying that he will come "when he has the opportunity" holds open the possibility that he will return at some stage, but for the moment the cliques have to resolve their difficulties without him.

Witherington goes on to give further insight into Paul's rhetorical strategy:

> It was good rhetorical strategy to leave Apollos's travel plans till the end of the letter, unlike the earlier references to Paul's own plans (cf. 4:17ff.), since this meant that Apollos's advocates would have to hear the whole of the letter's argument before they got their answer about their champion rhetor's plans. By then, Paul must have hoped that some of what he had said against factions based on Christian rhetors would have been accepted. In any case, he has done the best that he could do without actually being present to heal the rifts in the Corinthian congregation, and he intends to build on whatever success the letter might have with a personal visit, despite what "some" (4:18) may be thinking.[20]

Paul delayed speaking of Apollos' plans until the end of his letter because he knew that the clique claiming allegiance to Apollos would be disappointed at Apollos' reluctance to return immediately. This would have provided time, as Witherington conjectures, for the Corinthian cliques to think more about their positions in light of the arguments that Paul had made throughout his letter.

Noteworthy here is the way Paul speaks of Apollos. Displaying no antagonism, Paul refers to Apollos by the simple characteristic term of "brother," denoting the fictive kinship that is established in this Jesus group. From what we know about Paul from his other letters, if he did consider Apollos to blame for causing the divisions, he would have condemned him strongly. For example, Paul's letter to the Galatians shows strong objections to the actions of James and Peter. Paul identifies them by name and says clearly, "But when Cephas came to Antioch, I opposed him to his face, because he stood self-condemned" (Gal 2:11). Paul would have done the same regarding Apollos had he been responsible. But he did not.

Conclusion

This testimony from 1 Corinthians shows what a remarkable influence Apollos exerted upon the Corinthian Jesus group. In a cultural context where oratorical skills and philosophical eloquence were greatly revered, Apollos' stay in Corinth was received with great enthusiasm among some in the Jesus group, his "fans." It was in some ways parallel to the reception that Dio Chyrsostom himself records about his own appearance in Corinth. We have been at pains to stress that there is no evidence that Apollos intended to cause the Jesus group of Corinth to react in the way in which they did. It occurred spontaneously after he left. Nevertheless, the flip side to this clique formation around Apollos shows that some of the Jesus group of Corinth looked on Apollos as being on the same level and possessing the same abilities as some of the great orators, philosophers, and eloquent speakers who had ever graced the city of Corinth.

The clique formation is testimony to the regard in which Apollos was held by some of the Corinthian Jesus group. It is also testimony to his rhetorical skills and philosophical wisdom. Apollos emerges from this study as a thinker and a speaker, at home among the best of the rhetorical speakers and philosophical thinkers the Greek world had to offer.

In the next chapter, we will examine the recollections of Luke from the third Pauline generation. What we have deduced about Apollos from 1 Corinthians and his relationship to wisdom will be supported from the examination of these recollections in the Acts of the Apostles.

CHAPTER 4

Apollos of Alexandria: Third-Generation Recollections

In the previous chapter, we examined authentic information from the first Pauline generation about Apollos, gleaned from the first letter to the Corinthians. Apollos emerged as a change agent in his own right. He was an impressive speaker who attracted much attention (and allegiance) in Corinth. He worked in conjunction with Paul who proudly acknowledged him as a "brother," a fellow kinsman in the faith. In this capacity, he was associated with Paul's social network. In this chapter, our focus turns to the next written source about Apollos from the third Pauline generation. Around 90 CE, Luke, the writer of the Acts of the Apostles, presented recollections related to Paul's social network. This third Pauline generation was proud of the accomplishments of Paul and his colleagues. The Acts of the Apostles hands on these recollections in order to preserve the memory of their forefathers and foremothers who were their heroes in faith.

In writing the Acts of the Apostles in the third Pauline generation, Luke pays close attention to many of Paul's colleagues

who formed part of Paul's social network. Among these colleagues, Luke introduces recollections related to Apollos. It is
fascinating to see how these recollections fill in details related
to the picture of Apollos that we have already gleaned from 1
Corinthians. It supports as well the deductions we made that
Apollos must have been an impressive orator, whose wisdom
attracted a clique to form in his name.

First Corinthians is a high-context text. Paul introduced Apollos in his letter without explaining who he was, where he came
from, and so forth. Paul was concerned with resolving the issue
in Corinth—he presumed his readers were well aware of the
people to whom he made reference, such as Apollos. This is why
the recollections from the third generation are so important. Acts
18:24-28 provides much information about Apollos' origin and
background. It fills out many of the missing gaps.

These recollections lead us to examine the following aspects
that are helpful in understanding the person of Apollos. As a
first-century Mediterranean person, Apollos was embedded in
the house of Israel, lived in the Western Diaspora, and more
specifically in the city of Alexandria. He was well educated, and
the place of the synagogue was central to his role as change
agent. In this chapter, we will examine these further recollections
by situating them within the cultural, social, and historical world
of the end of the first century.

Diaspora

"Now there came to Ephesus a Jew named Apollos." (Acts 18:24)

Acts 18:24 introduces Apollos, situating him and his activity
within the context of the Hellenistic world. His activity in
Ephesus shows his focus on the Israelite community in the
Diaspora rather than the land of Israel.

The word Diaspora (from the Greek *diaspora*, meaning "dispersion")[1] became a technical term to refer to Israelite communities
that were settled outside the land of Judea. Today, for Zionist

political purposes, the term is used to refer to Jews who live outside modern Israel.[2] The legendary beginning of settlements of Israelites outside their homeland is attributed to a forced deportation of elite inhabitants after the conquest of the northern kingdom by the Assyrians in the eighth century BCE and of the southern kingdom of Judeans by the Babylonians in the sixth century BCE. Settlements of Judean communities in Egypt also began during the sixth century BCE for fear of the Babylonians. These Israelite-Judean settlements in Egypt were part of a voluntary movement, foreshadowing a steady migration in subsequent centuries from the homeland to other parts of the Mediterranean world as well as to areas east of Israel.

The term Diaspora tends to imply the idea of forced removal. Yet, most of the Israelites left their homeland voluntarily. Since the word Diaspora perpetuates a false understanding of what happened, John Pilch suggests using the term "colonies" to refer to those Israelites living outside the land of Israel.[3] Pilch derives this term from Philo, who refers to those who have been sent out from Judea and formed colonies throughout the Mediterranean world:

> Concerning the holy city I must now say what is necessary. It, as I have already stated, is my native country, and the metropolis, not only of the one country of Judaea, but also of many, by reason of the *colonies* which it has sent out from time to time into the bordering districts of Egypt, Phoenicia, Syria in general, and especially that part of it which is called Coelo-Syria, and also with those more distant regions of Pamphylia, Cilicia, the greater part of Asia Minor as far as Bithynia, and the furthermost corners of Pontus. And in the same manner into Europe, into Thessaly, and Boeotia, and Macedonia, and Aetolia, and Attica, and Argos, and Corinth and all the most fertile and wealthiest districts of Peoloponnesus. (*Embassy*, 281; emphasis added)

Colonies is a very appropriate way of referring to those Israelites living outside Israel since they had no intention of returning to their homeland. I shall follow Pilch's lead by using the terminology of colonies in place of Diaspora. The major difference between the Israelites living in these colonies and those remaining in their homeland was that the former lived in cities while the latter lived in small villages and agricultural areas. Living in colonies during the first century, the Hellenized Israelites were concentrated in the major cities of the Roman Empire, such as Alexandria, Antioch, and Rome. Because of their religious beliefs, they were exempt from military service in the Roman army, and were allowed to pay the temple tax to Jerusalem.

Arye Edrei and Doron Mendels,[4] two scholars from Tel Aviv University and the Hebrew University of Jerusalem, have made an interesting argument for "two distinct diasporas." In other words, they argue that the Israelite colonies that were established in the east were different and distinct from those established in the western Mediterranean. They write,

> The Jewish world during the Hellenistic period was noticeably dispersed. In addition to the center in the Land of Israel, there were diaspora communities in both the east and the west. The eastern diaspora extended from Trans-Jordan to Babylonia, and the western diaspora included Asia Minor, Greece, Italy and the Mediterranean islands. Most of the scholars who have dealt with the Jewish diaspora during this period have blurred the distinction between the eastern and western diasporas. . . . In this article, we wish to re-examine this topic, and to suggest that the distinction between the two diasporas was not only geographic, but actually reflected a much more substantive split. The centrality of Jerusalem and the Land of Israel as a unifying force was a significant factor in the Jewish world prior to the destruction of the Temple. This was not so after the destruction.[5]

While Edrei and Mendels focus largely on the period after the destruction of the temple in 70 CE, many of their observations also apply to the prior period of the Second Temple. Below is a

chart compiled from their insights as they relate to the period
of the first century in order to illustrate the clear distinctions
between the eastern and western colonies.[6] Since our attention
will be focused on the city of Alexandria in Egypt, I have deliberately included a column to illustrate that a careful reading
shows Alexandria and Egypt clearly at home in the world of the
western Mediterranean colonies.

Comparison of Israelite Colonies outside Judea

	Eastern Colonies	Alexandria and Egypt	Western Colonies
Language	Hebrew/Aramaic	Greek	Greek
Communications	Hierarchical system: Leadership Institutions and Bureaucracy	Flat system of communication: Did not include institutions of leadership as in Israel	Flat system of communication: Did not include institutions of leadership as in Israel
Literature: Two different communities on either side of Mediterranean Sea serviced by two diverse bodies of literature, distinct in terms of content, genre, language, worldview	Hebrew Bible	The Septuagint (including the Bible, Apocrypha, and Pseudepigrapha)	The Septuagint (including the Bible, Apocrypha, and Pseudepigrapha)

	Eastern Colonies	Alexandria and Egypt	Western Colonies
Temple and Jerusalem	Jerusalem was the center for the Israelite deity— it housed the temple, honored as the house of Israel's God; Bond to the temple maintained through payment of the temple tax	Same as in the eastern colonies	Same as in the eastern colonies
Ritual Baths	Present	No evidence	No evidence
Synagogue Inscriptions	In Hebrew; Reflects the Israelite focus on community	In Greek; Hellenistic focus on the individual donor	In Greek; Hellenistic focus on the individual donor
Oral Law	Strong focus	No knowledge of oral law *Philo:* His legal corpus demonstrates that he relied strongly on the LXX. He knew only the Israelite biblical sources through the LXX.	No knowledge of oral law *Josephus:* He makes numerous references to the Israelite law. *Pagan, Greek, and Latin literature* give the image of the Israelite as one who lives according to the laws of the Torah, but not the oral law.

	Eastern Colonies	Alexandria and Egypt	Western Colonies
Prayer Obligatory and set prayer is not mentioned in sources from the time of the temple, in the Apocrypha and Pseudepigrapha, in the writings of Philo or Josephus, or in the New Testament.	After destruction of the temple, Rabbis created a new prayer service—it became a set ritual for Israelites in the land of Israel and eastern colonies. The rabbis insisted on the use of pure Hebrew in the prayers and that they not be committed to writing; not translated.	Not present	Not present

The above chart shows that the Israelite colonies divided into two separate worlds, separated by language (Greek and Hebrew/ Aramaic), geography (west and east), and even sacred literatures (the translated Bible with the Apocrypha and Pseudepigrapha being used only in the west). Geographically, Alexandria and Egypt lay closer to the land of Judea with a trade route that ran through the two countries. Mention is also made of high priests during the time of Herod the Great who came from Alexandria. The second book of Maccabees begins (1:1-9 and 1:10–2:18) with two letters from the Judeans of Jerusalem and Judea to the Israelites of Egypt. All of the above would argue for a closer contact with the land of Judea. Nevertheless, the Hellenized Israelite colonies in Alexandria (and Egypt) were oriented toward other Hellenized Israelite colonies in the western Mediterranean world. This is supported from an analysis of the above chart showing the closeness and conformity of Alexandria (Egypt) to the world of the western Mediterranean colonies.[7]

The above discussion helps us to understand and situate the person of Apollos. The analysis of the two worlds of Israelite colonies places Apollos as an embedded Hellenized Israelite at home in the Mediterranean cultural world of Greece and Rome. The position of Alexandria, oriented to the western Mediterranean colonies, accounts well for the decision Apollos made to travel west and not east when he set out as a traveling Israelite preacher. He was more at home in the west with a common language (Greek), sacred literature (the Septuagint), and culture (Greco-Roman).

Alexandria

"a Jew named Apollos, a native of Alexandria.
He was an eloquent man, well-versed in the scriptures."
(Acts 18:24)

Luke's recollection noted above from the third Pauline generation would remind the readers of Apollos' social standing as "a native of Alexandria." As indicated before, identifying someone by their city was an acknowledgment that they had an elite status.

In this investigation, I wish to examine what we know about the city of Alexandria as a way of answering two questions related to Apollos: What would the reference to Apollos' place of origin convey to the first-century readers of the Acts of the Apostles? What insight does this reference give us into the person of Apollos himself? These recollections from the third Pauline generation not only fill in gaps that the first Pauline generation left out, but they also give insight into Apollos as a change agent within the Israelite Jesus groups.

The City

Since Alexandria was Apollos' home city, the question arises, what cultural and social aspects of the city contribute to our understanding of Apollos?

From the third century BCE until late antiquity, Alexandria was culturally the most important city in the Mediterranean. Tradition associates the foundation of this city to Alexander the Great on April 7, 331 BCE. The city bordered the Mediterranean coastline of Egypt on the north, Lake Mareotis on the south, while the Nile Delta was to the east. The Egyptian name for the city was *Rakotis* (which means "Construction Site"), indicating that the city was built over a previous city that had been destroyed. This name continued to be associated with an area south of the city where the native Egyptian inhabitants of the city lived.

After Alexander's death, Alexandria became the capital of the new Ptolemaic state. However, it continued to be organized along the lines of a Greek city-state (such as Athens) with a citizen population made up of Greeks. Since Apollos was a Hellenized Israelite, he was not a citizen of Alexandria as this was reserved for ethnic Greeks, thus excluding both Israelites and Egyptians. Even though it was the capital of Egypt, Alexandria was always viewed as somewhat separate from Egypt itself as can be seen from its usual designation as *Alexandria ad Aegyptum* which literally means "Alexandria by Egypt."

The city probably comprised some half a million people at the time of Apollos. It was divided into five "quarters" each one designated by the first five letters of the Greek alphabet. At the time of Apollos, a sizable population of Hellenized Israelites occupied one of the entire sectors Delta, while a large number occupied part of another sector, Beta. This meant that the city comprised three distinct ethnic groups, Greek citizens, native Egyptians, and people originating from Israel/Judea.

Trade was an essential dimension of the city of Alexandria due to two natural harbors that graced the geography of the city: the Great Harbor to the east and the Western Harbor. They were separated by the *Heptastadium* (a man-made dyke) constructed from the mainland to the island of Pharos (where the Pharos Lighthouse stood, one of the seven wonders of the ancient world).[8] Alexandria was responsible for the transport of grain from Egypt to Rome. It was also a center for the production of papyrus and jewelry and mosaics, while spices and perfumes came there from Arabia and the East.

Cultural Institutions

Luke's third-generation Pauline recollections of Apollos identify him as "an eloquent man, well-versed in the scriptures" (Acts 18:24). As someone who was well educated, Apollos must have been very familiar with the cultic institutions of Alexandria. The most famous institutions, not only of Alexandria but also of the Hellenistic world, were the Museum and the Great Library. When Ptolemy I became the king of Egypt in 304 BCE, he established the Museum as a research center. Ptolemaic rulers invited scholars to study there, providing them with free accommodation, a stipend, and the use of the Great Library housed next to the Museum. This was the start of state-subsidized learning! The first truly scientific approach to research began there. Alexandria's scholarly reputation spread throughout the Mediterranean world.

The Great Library was built near the Museum. It soon became more important than the Museum and was one of the greatest cultural achievements of the ancient world. During the course of the third century BCE, under the leadership of Ptolemy II Philadelphus, a remarkable attempt was made to house the world's great literature by both honest and dishonest means alike. There is a story about Ptolemy III Euergetes (246–222 BCE, the third ruler of the Ptolemaic Dynasty) confiscating manuscripts from foreign travelers entering Alexandria. He would have these manuscripts copied, keeping the originals for the Library, and returning the copies to the travelers! Most of our knowledge of the Library comes from the *Letter of Aristeas* (200–170 BCE), which tells of the Greek translation of the Hebrew Scriptures under Ptolemy II. Many of the details concerning the account are apocryphal, as is probably the reference to the size of the Library itself as containing some 500,000 to 700,000 scrolls. Marc Antony is reported to have donated some 200,000 manuscripts to the Library that were taken from the competing Library in Pergamum.

The first librarian, Zenodotus (from 284 BCE), was called a *grammatikos* (a specialist of *grammata* [documents]), a corrector or an editor. He produced the first critical edition of Homer's works, which was the standard text until recently. Another librarian, Callimachus, was concerned with using the information at hand to compile catalogues of information about scrolls and other documents in the Library. He produced the *Tables* (of authors who proved themselves illustrious in all aspects of culture and in their writings) in 108 volumes. In 245 BCE another scholar, Eratosthenes, was appointed by Ptolemy III to take charge of the Library; he referred to himself as a philologist. He was a philosopher who was interested in different branches of learning, such as mathematics, astronomy, geography, literature, and history. He also wrote the *Chronographies*, which were chronological tables that traced the years of Greek history from the Trojan War to the death of Alexander the Great.

The Library of Alexandria made it possible to view the world from its own standpoint. It aimed at containing all Greek wisdom with the consequence that Alexandria became the center of learning in the ancient world. It was famous for its discoveries in fields ranging from astronomy to mathematics and physics. It had a world-famous reputation as a medical center. As a philosophical center, Alexandria replaced Athens in the first century BCE. In 86 BCE, Sulla partly destroyed Athens for supporting Mithridates VI Eupator Dionysus (king of Pontus in northern Anatolia, 120–63 BCE) in the war against Rome. Many philosophers left Athens for Alexandria, which soon became a prestigious center especially for Platonic philosophy in the first century. This was the city Apollos called home. Among the third-generation Pauline recollections, his origin in Alexandria was held in high regard. It pointed to his connection with the cultural center of the ancient world, which in turn would have conveyed to the readers of the Acts of the Apostles that he was a man of cultural, intellectual, and philosophical training.

The Hellenized Israelite Community

The third Pauline generation's first recollection about Apollos is his ethnic identity. He was an Israelite born in Alexandria. Consequently, an examination of the Hellenized Israelite community in Alexandria will help to give a clearer understanding of Apollos' ethnic background.

Israelite immigration into Egypt from Israel began at the end of the sixth century BCE. Writing against one of Israel's enemies, Josephus notes that Alexander himself settled Israelites in Alexandria and the numbers steadily grew. Josephus goes on to add:

> His [Apion's] astonishment at the idea of Jews [Judeans] being called Alexandrians betrays similar stupidity. All persons invited to join a colony, however different their nationality, take the name of the founders. (*Against Apion*, 2.38)

Of all the Israelite colonies in the Mediterranean world, we are best informed about those in Alexandria and Egypt. The largest Israelite colonies in the eastern Mediterranean were to be found in Egypt. Philo notes that there were as many as one million people of Israelite descent in Egypt (*Flaccus*, 43), and a large number of these were to be found in Alexandria. While this may be somewhat of an exaggeration, nevertheless it does point to the large number of Hellenized Israelites in Egypt. As noted above, the Israelite community lived together in two quarters of the city where they had been granted the special privilege of organizing themselves as a *politeuma* (or community; see *Letter of Aristeas*, 310). The Israelite community treasured their Sacred Writings and the traditions that emanated from them that formed their group identity. The bond that cemented the people together was their ethnic identity as Israelites. It gave them a sense of who they were and with whom they were connected. While preserving their ethnic identity as Israelites, they spoke Greek and were strongly attracted to and influenced by the Hellenistic culture of Alexandria and the Mediterranean, which they absorbed and treasured.

Erich Gruen has examined well the position and situation of the Hellenized Israelites in Alexandria.[9] In focusing on the pogrom of 38 CE, he shows that this planned campaign of persecution was really an isolated incident, initiated by Egyptians (not the ethnic Greeks) against the Hellenized Israelites. His summary sets out very clearly and succinctly the position of Hellenized Israelites in the city of Alexandria. It also illuminates what must have been the experience of Apollos in Alexandria:

> The experience of Jews in Alexandria from the founding of the city to the advent of the Great Revolt—nearly four full centuries—was a predominantly positive one. Jews played a full part in the social, economic, and cultural life of Ptolemaic Alexandria. Their religious institutions and traditions had official sanction and express support from both Ptolemies and Roman emperors. They enjoyed civic privileges together with their own political organs and officialdom. Juridical "citizenship," whatever that might mean, held no special appeal; it was neither an object of desire nor a source of conflict. The Jews were "Alexandrians." In short, the dreadful pogrom of 38 in no way defines or exemplifies the history of Jews in Alexandria. . . . Concentration on that grim episode has distorted the broader history: a lengthy and productive relationship between Jews and Greeks, and the rich and rewarding experience of the Jews in the city of Alexandria.[10]

This was the ethnic group in which Apollos was embedded. Born and educated in Alexandria, he was fully part of the Hellenized Israelite community that lived together in two of the sectors of the city. He did not possess citizenship in the city since it was reserved solely to the ethnic Greek population. This was no hindrance to his relationship with the Greek population, and he would have clearly viewed himself fully as an Alexandrian.

The Septuagint

The third Pauline generation recollects that Apollos was "well-versed in the scriptures" (Acts 18:24). The Scriptures that Apollos used were the Septuagint (literally "seventy," and abbreviated as LXX), which refers to the Greek translation of the Hebrew Scriptures. The name comes from the story in the *Letter of Aristeas*, which tells of the origin of the Greek translation of the Hebrew Bible. The story narrates how King Ptolemy (probably Ptolemy II Philadelphus [285–247 BCE]) wanting to acquire all the books in the world, learned that the laws of the Israelites were not among his collection. He consequently wrote to the high priest in Jerusalem requesting that six learned elders from each tribe of the Israelites should be sent to Alexandria to complete the task of translating the Torah into Greek. When the elders arrived in Alexandria they were given comfortable accommodations beside the sea where they completed the task of translating the Torah within seventy-two days. The Egyptian king was highly impressed with the translation and the mind of the Lawgiver. The story has given the name to the Greek translation from the reference to seventy-two translators as well as to the seventy-two days in which it was completed.

Originally the term referred only to the Greek translation of the Torah, the first five books of the Hebrew Scriptures. As time went by, the remaining books of the Hebrew Scriptures were translated into Greek, namely the Prophets and the other writings. These Greek translations, comprising the thirty-nine books of the Hebrew Bible, were also included under the name Septuagint. At the same time, other writings either written in Alexandria itself or translated into Greek from a Hebrew original were incorporated under this term Septuagint. The translator of the book of Ecclesiasticus (or Sirach) illustrates this point by telling us in his prologue how he translated the work of his grandfather from Hebrew into Greek:

> Many great teachings have been given to us through the
> Law and the Prophets and the others that followed them,

and for these we should praise Israel for instruction and wisdom. Now, those who read the scriptures must not only themselves understand them, but must also as lovers of learning be able through the spoken and written word to help the outsiders. So my grandfather Jesus, who had devoted himself especially to the reading of the Law and the Prophets and the other books of our ancestors, and had acquired considerable proficiency in them, was himself also led to write something pertaining to instruction and wisdom, so that by becoming familiar also with his book those who love learning might make even greater progress in living according to the law.

You are invited therefore to read it with goodwill and attention, and to be indulgent in cases where, despite our diligent labor in translating, we may seem to have rendered some phrases imperfectly.

The writings belonging to the Septuagint, then, include the Greek translation of the thirty-nine books in the Hebrew canon, as well as seven other works, namely the books of Judith, Tobit, Baruch, Wisdom, Ecclesiasticus (or Sirach), 1 and 2 Maccabees, together with additions to the books of Esther and Daniel. These seven books are recognized as deuterocanonical Scripture by the Roman Catholic, Greek, and Russian Orthodox Churches. Some ancient manuscripts also include a few other books such as 1 Esdras, the Psalms of Solomon (in the Codex Vaticanus from the fourth century CE), and 3 and 4 Maccabees (in the Codex Alexandrinus from the fifth century CE).

The importance of the Septuagint cannot be overestimated. It was the Bible of the early Jesus groups. When the recollections of the third Pauline generation in Acts 18:24 state that Apollos was "well-versed in the scriptures," the reference is to the Septuagint (namely, the Greek translation of the Hebrew Scriptures as well as those extra writings that it included). These recollections show that Apollos was remembered as someone who had great learning in the Sacred Scriptures. His preaching and wisdom must have been based as well on the Scriptures. Not only did Apollos use this translation, but Paul and all the other New Testament writers have been shown to have used this translation as well. It stands to reason that since the New Testament writers were writing for Jesus groups living in western Israelite colonies outside Judea, they would use their Greek text, the Septuagint.

Philo

The Hellenized Israelite community of Alexandria was greatly influenced by the intellectual and scholarly context of the city. This is most notable in the works of the Hellenized Israelite philosopher, Philo (20 BCE–50 CE). An older contemporary of Apollos, Philo used Platonic and Stoic philosophy to explain and make the Septuagint understandable for his fellow Alexandrian Israelites. Since the Hellenized Israelite community spoke Greek, lived in a Greek city (Alexandria), breathed Greek culture and thought patterns, clearly Philo needed to interpret the Septuagint in terms of the thought patterns and philosophy of the Greek world. A noteworthy aspect of his thinking was the extensive use he made of allegory in his interpretation of the Septuagint. Further, he identified the personification of Wisdom with the Greek concept of Logos.

Since Apollos and Philo both came from the same city and were contemporaries, it is logical to presume that Apollos either knew Philo or at least was familiar with his thinking and writings. Given that Apollos was also "well-versed in the scriptures" (Acts 18:24), it can be further conjectured that his understanding of these Scriptures must have been influenced by Philo's philosophy and teachings. No wonder the Jesus group of Corinth was impressed by his rhetoric as well as his philosophical wisdom in explaining the Scriptures!

The Synagogue

"[Apollos] began to speak boldly in the synagogue." (Acts 18:26)

The third-generation Pauline recollections show that the first institution Apollos sought out when he arrived in Ephesus was the synagogue. Clearly familiar with this institution from Alexandria, Apollos sought to connect with the one institution that gave expression to his Israelite ethnic identity. An examination of this institution, called the "synagogue," is significant for three reasons: in the first instance, it helps us to avoid the anachronistic fallacy of considering the synagogue as if it were the same institution as today; second, it helps us recognize the difference between the Israelites living in the land of Israel and Hellenized Israelites living in colonies throughout the Mediterranean; and third, it helps us appreciate the significance of a center that fostered and promoted ethnic Israelite identity, especially for those who lived outside the homeland. The synagogue would also have served as a center for the gathering of the Jesus groups.

Egyptian and Alexandrian Synagogues

For Jewish people today, a synagogue is essentially a place of worship where every Sabbath a prayer service is conducted with a discernible and distinctive structure. It is important to avoid the anachronistic fallacy whereby we retrofit a twenty-first-century synagogue onto the past. Instead, evidence from the first century must be allowed to speak for itself.

Significant evidence has emerged from Hellenized Israelite communities in Egypt and more specifically in Alexandria regarding early institutions that were designated by the Greek term *proseuchē*.[11] What exactly is indicated by this word? This term is often translated as "synagogue," but this simply perpetuates the anachronistic fallacy mentioned above. The Greek word *proseuchē* literally means "place of prayer."[12] But, it is also misleading to translate the word in this way as it introduces an idea into these places that the evidence does not support, as we shall see. The answer lies in examining with an open mind the evidence that has emerged from a study of epigraphical material and papyrological manuscripts from the period prior to 70 CE, the period of Apollos. This is an interesting and revealing exploration. I shall refer to these institutions by this Greek term *proseuchē* to avoid perpetuating the anachronistic fallacy by referring to them as synagogues or as places of prayer.

Hellenized Israelite communities in the western Mediterranean colonies, especially in Alexandria and Egypt, have provided scholars with a rich source of information for the Israelite *proseuchē*. The epigraphical evidence dates to as early as the third century BCE, while papyrological information comes from the first century BCE. One of the most surprising facts of all is that while there is a fairly substantial amount of evidence from Egypt and Alexandria there is almost no evidence whatsoever from either epigraphical or papyrological sources relating to the existence of such centers in Syria. Only limited evidence is available for such centers in Greece, Italy, and Asia Minor.

While no building has been discovered in Egypt for this pre-70 CE period, epigraphical material has helped clarify the meaning of this term *proseuchē*.[13] The following are two examples of dedicatory inscriptions found in Egypt from the Ptolemaic period:

> "On behalf of king Ptolemy and Berenice his sister and wife and their children, the Jews (dedicated) the *proseuchē*."[14] (italics mine)

> "On behalf of king Ptolemy and queen Cleopatra the sister and queen Cleopatra the wife, Benefactors, the Jews in Nitriai (dedicated) the *proseuchē* and its appurtenances."[15] (italics mine)

These inscriptions illustrate the custom of dedicating these institutions to the royal family. This indicates the loyalty of the Hellenized Israelite community toward the royal family as well as their dependence on it. Dedicatory plaques and inscriptions were not unique to the Israelites in Alexandria. It seems that the Hellenized Israelite community of Alexandria was following a pervasive Greek custom. As Fraser says, "The most abundant single source for the study of Alexandrian religion is the dedicatory plaques set up in shrines, public or private, in honor of a particular deity."[16] In following this Greek custom, the Israelite inscriptions adapted them to conform to their customary beliefs. They naturally omitted any reference to a particular deity, but preserved "'a loyalty formula': the dedication begins with the words 'On behalf of King Ptolemy and the Queen.'"[17]

That the *proseuchē* had a specifically religious function is evident from the words used to refer to them. A number of inscriptions used the phrase "holy" or "great place." One such *proseuchē* dated to the end of the second century BCE is identified in this way:

> On the orders of the queen and king, in place of the previous plaque about the dedication of the *proseuchē*, let what is written below be written up: King Ptolemy Euergetes (proclaimed) the *proseuchē* inviolate [(*asulon*)]. The queen and king gave the order.[18] (italics mine)

Philo's writings are also very informative for understanding the Alexandrian *proseuchē*. Philo's terminology is revealing: on nineteen occasions he uses the term *proseuchē*,[19] while he uses the term *synagogē* only twice. Philo also uses words that indicate the holiness of the place (such as *temenos* [consecrated ground], *hieroi periboloi* [sacred places]).[20] Most characteristic of Philo's writings is his reference to the *proseuchē* as a school (*didaskaleion*) with its focus on the reading of and instruction in the sacred texts.[21] Another interesting observation Philo makes is that the *proseuchē* was also a place where the contributions to the temple tax were housed until they could be brought to Jerusalem. Philo goes to great length to describe one *proseuchē*: he indicates that it was large in size, and very ornately decorated with, among other things, shields, golden crowns, and inscriptions to the emperor.[22] Philo probably singles out these decorations as a way of pointing out to the emperor how loyal the Hellenized Israelites were to the Romans. This was especially important at the time of a pogrom conducted in 38 CE against the Hellenized Israelites.

Proseuchē *in the Western Mediterranean Colonies:* The Synagogue in Judea

While Alexandria and Egypt made reference to the *proseuchē*, Judea during the first century made reference to the synagogue. Some twenty synagogues are referred to in literary sources, such as in the writings of Josephus (Tiberias, Dor, and Caesarea), the New Testament (Nazareth, Capernaum, and Jerusalem), Rabbinic Literature (Jerusalem), and the Damascus Document (Qumran). In addition, four sites dating back to the first century have produced clear archaeological evidence for the existence of synagogues. Once again, we must remember that while the term "synagogue" is used in these documents and on these inscriptions, it must not be confused with the modern day synagogue. Much discussion has taken place among scholars about the purpose of synagogues in Judea prior to the destruction of the temple in 70 CE. A careful reading of the famous Theodotos inscription makes it possible to discover the main function of the synagogue in Judea in the first century.

This Theodotos inscription was found in a cistern in 1913–14 during excavations of the City of David by the French archaeologist, Raymond Weill. Written in Greek, and dated to the first century, this stone inscription reads as follows:

> Theodotos, the son of Vettenos, priest and *archisynagogos*, son of an *archisynagogos*, grandson of an *archisynagogos*, built this synagogue [*tēn synagōgēn*] for the reading of the Law [i.e., the Torah] and the study of the commandments, and a guesthouse and rooms and water installations for hosting those in need from abroad, it [i.e., the synagogue], having been founded by his fathers, the presbyters, and Simonides.[23]

This Theodotos inscription associates three activities with the synagogue: the reading of the law (or Torah), the studying of the commandments, and the provision of accommodation and water for travelers. Most noteworthy of all is that no reference is made to prayer services as such. This should not be surprising since the center for Israelite prayer and worship was the temple. Pilgrimages were organized to Jerusalem and the temple for the three great festivals in the Israelite political religious calendar: Passover (Pesach), Pentecost (Shavuot), and Booths (Sukkoth). The evolution of the synagogue throughout Judea was chiefly as a center for the activities of the local communities. Lee Levine argues that the city gate used to be the place for holding gatherings of the local community.[24] This role was taken over by the synagogue. Local people would have gathered especially for the reading and study of the law as well as for providing a place to meet the needs of the local community.

This means that the *proseuchē* in Alexandria and Egypt and the synagogue in Judea emerged at more or less the same time in the first few centuries BCE. Their origin, purpose, and function, however, differed greatly. In Judea, the function of the developing synagogue was to offer a place where community activities could take place. In Alexandria and Egypt, the Hellenized Israelites needed a place where they could give expression to their identity in an alien environment. The *proseuchē* was the way Israelite identity was forged and handed on from one generation to the next.

The question still remains: did communal worship and prayer take place in the synagogue and the *proseuchē*? The answer to this question must be given separately regarding the synagogue and the *proseuchē*. As regards the synagogue, the place and role of the temple in Judea would have precluded the synagogue becoming a place of worship and communal prayer. That role was reserved for the temple. So while the temple existed, there was no need for the synagogue to provide this function. After the temple's destruction the synagogue was poised to assume this role. There is no evidence to show that the synagogue in pre-70 CE Judea was a place for prayer. Quite the contrary! The evidence points to it being a place for communal activities among which the reading of the law was the most distinctive element.

In Alexandria and Egypt (and the rest of the western Mediterranean colonies) the situation was very different from that of Judea. The name given to their gathering places, *proseuchē*, as we indicated before, literally means "a place of prayer." But, why was this name given to these Israelite institutions when the reading and explanation of the Torah was the central activity that occurred there?

Lee Levine has given a plausible explanation for this discrepancy between the central activity taking place, namely the reading of the Torah or Sacred Scriptures, and the name *proseuchē*. Levine has argued that Greco-Roman political religious ceremonies exerted an influence on these Hellenized Israelite *proseuchē*.[25] In the Greco-Roman political religious ceremonies, the use of hymns and prayers formed an important part. It would have been natural for the Hellenized Israelite communities in Alexandria and elsewhere in the western Mediterranean colonies to imitate these ceremonies by employing hymns and prayers in the context of their own services when they gathered to read and study the Torah. Their great distance from the political and religious center of the temple gave an impetus to the communities in Alexandria and throughout the western Mediterranean colonies to develop and foster their own identity through the development of their own patterns of worship. The name *proseuchē* would have pointed to this, and it would also have given their institutions a sense of the holy that was to be honored and respected.

In summary, we can say that the *proseuchē* in Alexandria and Egypt and the synagogue in Judea emerged independently yet at more or less the same time in the first few centuries BCE. As has been shown above, their origin, purpose, and function differed as a result of very different social contexts and the influences that these contexts placed on them. In Judea, the temple was the religious center and heart of the nation, hence the synagogue was careful not to usurp any of its functions, especially that of its central activity of communal worship. In the western Mediterranean colonies, on the other hand, the Israelites were living in the midst of non-Israelites and non-Israelite forms of worship. This distinctive context necessitated the Israelites developing an institution (the *proseuchē*) in which they could preserve and deepen their own identity with an ethnic expression centered on the Torah since they were so far removed from their worship center, the temple.

This detailed explanation of the *proseuchē* in Alexandria helps us appreciate the significance of a center that fostered and promoted the ethnic Israelite identity, especially for those who lived outside the homeland. It is essential for understanding the reference to Apollos' activity in the Ephesian *proseuchē*, "he began to speak boldly in the synagogue" (Acts 18:26). Apollos' familiarity with this central institution of his ethnic group in Alexandria would have been the bond that drew him to the same institution in Ephesus.

Apollos:
Embedded within the Cultural World of Alexandria

"He was an eloquent man." (Acts 18:24)

When the third-generation Pauline recollections present Apollos, as "a Hellenized Israelite . . . a native of Alexandria," they highlight Apollos as embedded in two worlds: cultural Hellenistic Alexandria and the ethnic Hellenized Israelite community. The purpose of the previous section's detailed examination of Alexandria was to illustrate precisely how Apollos as "a native of Alexandria" (Acts 18:24) was embedded within both these worlds: the social and cultural context of the world of Alexandria and the ethnic world of the Hellenized Israelite community. In this present section, we wish to examine specifically what was undoubtedly the most significant cultural influence on Apollos, namely his rhetorical education.

As a native of Alexandria, Apollos was embedded in the greatest cultural center of the Hellenistic world. His line of vision was outward to the countries and cities of the Mediterranean world, not inward toward Egypt. He would have been steeped in the culture of Alexandria itself.

The third-generation Pauline recollections focus on Apollos' ability to communicate and speak well: "he was an eloquent man" (Acts 18:24). In Greek culture from the beginning of recorded time, an ability to speak well was identified as one of the defining characteristics for every cultivated person. Even in the Hellenic warrior ethos, the ability to fight on the battlefield went side by side with the ability to speak well. In Homer's *Iliad* we see how the fighting prowess of Achilles and Hector was matched by their ability to deliver speeches and to communicate well with their men. In the context of Hellenistic society where people gathered to discuss and enact their laws, an ability to speak well was one of the most important gifts one could possess. The whole education system revolved around providing training in the art of rhetoric, the art of persuasion. Apollos belonged to that Alexandrian culture encapsulated in the spirit of the Library and the Museum. As an inhabitant of Alexandria, Apollos would have been imbued with the same spirit of learning and acquiring knowledge.

Although we have no record of any speech delivered or written by Apollos, nevertheless, we are able to make some good conjectures about Apollos in this regard from the knowledge that we have gained of the Hellenized Israelite community of Alexandria. D. F. Watson has commented that "many Jews of the upper class were anxious for their children to have a Hellenistic education, while others preferred the traditional Jewish education, considering the influence of the polytheistic nature of Greek instruction to be a danger to faith."[26] Alexandria would have been the most sought after center for those Israelites outside Judea who wanted their children to receive a Hellenistic education. We can imagine that Apollos would have been trained in the foundation of all Hellenistic education, namely rhetoric or the art of persuasion. Since Alexandria was the center of the cultural world during the first century, it stands to reason that Apollos, as an elite member of the Israelite community in Alexandria, would have been well trained in the art of rhetoric. What exactly would this training or education in rhetoric entail?

Only in recent times has attention been devoted to the examination of rhetoric in the context of the world of the New Testament and its writings. Over the past few decades, different attempts have been made to look at the importance of the study of rhetoric for appreciating the New Testament. Vernon Robbins has been at the forefront of arguing for a more detailed study of rhetoric by New Testament scholars.[27]

Bruce Malina, Jerome Neyrey, and other members of the group involved with the social-science study of the New Testament have also given detailed attention to discovering new ways that would allow us to see how "ancient Mediterraneans thought of each other."[28]

From the third Pauline generation the dominant recollection of Apollos is that he was "an eloquent man" (Acts 18:24). With this as my starting point, I wish to examine what that might mean in the cultural social context of a first-century Mediterranean person from Alexandria. By using the above studies and approaches, I wish to focus on what we can deduce and apply to Apollos regarding his rhetorical education and how he would have been "perceived and described" by others, to use the language of Malina and Neyrey.

Two sources for our knowledge of ancient rhetoric exist. In the first place, standard textbooks (or *technai*) were designed for scholars and teachers who had a detailed understanding of rhetoric. Among the extant textbooks are the following: Aristotle's *Rhetorica ad Alexandrum* and the *Rhetorica*; the *Rhetorica ad Herennium*, and some writings by Cicero, such as *De Inventione*, *De Optimo Genere Oratorum*, *Topica*, *De Oratore*, *De Partitione Oratoriae*, and *Orator*. As Burton Mack comments, "Thus these handbooks presupposed not only an advanced level of proficiency in rhetorical training, but a high level of general education and readership in the canons of literature as well."[29]

A look at the *Rhetorica ad Herennium*, the standard textbook of the time, is most informative. It identifies three types of public speaking, namely, the epideictic (the praise or criticism of someone), the deliberative (which considers a specific topic and aims at persuading or dissuading the audience), and the judicial (which occurs in the context of a courtroom) (*Ad Her.*, 1.2, 2). The *Ad Herennium* becomes more detailed in that it outlines five elements needed for a complete argument and illustrates how a theme (or thesis) is developed in seven steps.[30] We can see reflected in the *Ad Herennium* techniques or methods that Apollos would have received in his training and education in rhetoric and public speaking. The *Ad Herennium* was written in Latin during the first century BCE and reflected the Greek rhetorical tradition. I am in no way arguing that Apollos either knew or used this treatise. I am simply referring to the *Ad Herennium* because it provides an example of the basics of Greek rhetorical art being used throughout the Mediterranean world. It gives us a wonderful example and insight into the type of rhetoric in which Apollos was trained.

Another source for our knowledge of ancient rhetoric comes from the *progymnasmata*, or exercise books. These were produced for students, giving them the tools and examples needed to master the art of rhetoric. Theon's *Progymnasmata* (coming from the first century) is the most ancient text of this genre that we possess today. Without doubt many other such *progymnasmata* predated this work but have been lost. These *progymnasmata* were what we today would term exercise books. These books provided students with models and examples of how to write (and would have been applied to their speeches as well). The aim was to perform again what had been presented to them, to imitate by performing it in their own words. Originality did not embrace novel ideas (as we view originality today). Instead, originality consisted of the way in which a person used the accepted methods of presenting material. Education in rhetoric was above all directed toward conformity to and mastery of these accepted ways through practice and exercises. This clearly was the education that Apollos would have received in Alexandria.

In summary, the recollections of the third Pauline generation of Apollos as "an eloquent man" (Acts 18:24) open up for us a way of understanding Apollos within the social and cultural world of the first-century Mediterranean. By situating these recollections within this social and cultural world, we have been able to construct an insight into the remarkable rhetorical education and training that Apollos would have received in Alexandria—a rhetorical education that was the best in the Hellenistic world of the first century. It would have paralleled the education that a student would expect to receive today at a first-rate university. At the same time, as a Hellenized Israelite, we can imagine that his education would also have been influenced by the thinking of Philo. From him, he would have learned how to understand the Israelite traditions in the thought patterns of Platonic and Stoic thought. Apollos emerges as a real person whose rhetorical skills would have provided him with tremendous abilities to become an effective change agent in spreading the gospel of the God of Israel proclaimed by Paul, as we will note below.

Apollos: Alexandria to Ephesus

"Priscilla and Aquila . . . took [Apollos] aside
and explained the Way of God to him more accurately." (Acts 18:26)

The third-generation Pauline recollections in the Acts of the Apostles indicate that Apollos went from Alexandria to Ephesus where he conducted his preaching "in the synagogue" (18:26). Although no archaeological evidence has yet been provided for a synagogue in Ephesus, many other centers in Asia Minor have yielded archaeological evidence for synagogues that conform to what has been presented here with similarities to the *proseuchē* in Alexandria. On this basis, we would deduce that the Hellenized Israelite community in Ephesus would also have possessed a *proseuchē* similar to all the other centers of the western Mediterranean.

As we argued in our examination of the *proseuchē* in Alexandria, the central activity was the reading of the Torah and the subsequent commentary on the text that had been read. When journeying to another city in the Hellenistic world, it would have been natural for Apollos to seek out that center within the city that provided hospitality to a fellow Israelite. It likewise provided an opportunity for Hellenized Israelites to gather, to express their identity through hearing the reading and study of their sacred texts. Apollos gravitated toward that institution with which he was familiar in order to share his understanding of "the Way of the Lord" (18:25).

Paul did exactly the same thing when he journeyed to a new town or city—he always sought out the local synagogue. Paul's visit to Antioch of Pisidia (Acts 13:13-52) is a perfect example of his custom of finding the local synagogue so that he could proclaim his message. Noteworthy again in this context is the way in which Luke describes the gathering. It conforms exactly to what we have described above regarding the gathering in the *proseuchē*. The focus rested on the reading of the Scriptures and their explanation: "After the reading of the law and the prophets, the officials of the synagogue sent them a message, saying, 'Brothers, if you have any word of exhortation for the people, give it.' So Paul stood up and with a gesture began to speak" (Acts 13:15-16).

From these third-generation Pauline recollections, we can deduce that Apollos had gained an understanding of John the Baptist's teaching regarding Jesus as the Messiah (Acts 18:25). Apollos was excited about this new understanding, "he spoke with burning enthusiasm" (Acts 18:25). He desired to spread this message across the Mediterranean world.

On leaving Alexandria, it would have been logical for Apollos to head first for Ephesus, the capital of the Province of Asia. The emperor Augustus (27 BCE–14 CE) had established Ephesus as the capital of the Roman province of Asia, which began a new period of prosperity for the city with the construction of many buildings. From Ephesus, Apollos would have had the opportunity to spread his message to the rest of the cities and towns of Asia. Strabo (*Geography*, 641–42) notes that the geographical location of Ephesus contributed to its significance and importance. Not only did it have a wonderful location on the Aegean Sea, it also formed part of the vast Anatolian highway system that Strabo describes in these words, "There is a kind of common road constantly used by all who travel from Ephesus towards the east" (*Geography*, 663). At the time of Apollos, all the trade routes of Asia converged on Ephesus and the Romans used Ephesus as the starting point for measuring distances from Asia. These facts explain further the reasons that brought Apollos to Ephesus: from there it would have been easy to travel farther to spread his message.

The third Pauline generation gives additional recollections about Apollos when Acts 18:25 says that he had "been instructed in the Way of the Lord." Luke had referred before to Jesus-group members as belonging to "the Way" when he mentioned Saul's intent to persecute them (Acts 9:2). The content of Apollos' knowledge and preaching regarding "the Way of the Lord" was limited, as Acts 18:25 further explains: "[H]e knew only the baptism of John." Specifically, Apollos had only heard of the beginning of Jesus' ministry insofar as John the Baptist had identified Jesus as Israel's Messiah. In his preaching, Apollos would have used the Scriptures to explain his basic understanding of Jesus as Messiah.

Priscilla and Aquila "heard him [Apollos] . . . and explained the Way of God to him more accurately" (Acts 18:26). Priscilla and Aquila, members of the Jesus group of Ephesus, heard Apollos speaking in the synagogue. They explained to him more fully about God's agency in the resurrected Jesus as Messiah, soon to restore Israel's theocracy: with God as Israel's ruler and the liberation of the land of Judea from the domination of the foreign rulers, the Romans.

As a traveling Israelite, Apollos intended to journey from Ephesus to Achaia (Acts 18:27). Because Apollos' time with Priscilla and Aquila gave him a more accurate understanding of "the Way of God" in the resurrected Jesus, the members of the Jesus group of Ephesus "wrote to the disciples to welcome him" (Acts 18:27). They provided him with a letter of recommendation, a common strategy among the Jesus groups (as can be seen from 2 Cor 3:1; Rom 16:1; Col 4:10). Such letters of recommendation were vital in the ancient world, introducing the stranger to the community and requesting hospitality for him.

Hospitality was probably the central virtue people in the Mediterranean world were expected to practice. Once again the danger of anachronism must be avoided in approaching this value. In our world, hospitality is generally associated with "entertaining family and friends."[31] However, in the world of the Mediterranean hospitality dealt with foreigners or strangers (*xenoi*). Bruce Malina and John Pilch[32] have given a detailed understanding of the significance and obligations required by hospitality in the Mediterranean world. They note that three stages can be observed in the exercise of the value of hospitality:

- *Strangers are tested* because they pose a threat to the community. The letter of recommendation often replaces the testing since strangers have been vouched for by the sender of the letter. The letter tells the Jesus-group members that this stranger does not need to be tested because he belongs to their group, their fictive kin.

- *The stranger enters a new relationship*: He becomes a guest in the home of the host. This means that the host is obliged to protect and care for the guest.

- *The guest leaves the home of the host either as friend or enemy.* As a friend, the relationship continues to endure. The theme of hospitality is also central in the poems of Homer. *The Iliad* shows the consequences of the betrayal of hospitality. The Trojan War was provoked by Paris who broke the rules of hospitality by abducting Menelaus' wife, Helen. The intent of the war was to restore honor to Menelaus who had been insulted through this action. The story of *The Odyssey* is also a story of hospitality, honored or broken.[33]

These recollections provided by Luke from the third Pauline generation throw light on the conflict in the first Pauline generation in 1 Corinthians as they are understood in the framework of the cultural and social world of the first century.

Apollos: Ephesus to Corinth as Change Agent

*"On his arrival [in Corinth Apollos] greatly helped
those who through grace had become believers." (Acts 18:27)*

Apollos left Alexandria for Ephesus as a traveling teacher with a certain knowledge of Jesus as Messiah in relationship to John and his baptism (Acts 18:24-25). John's task had been to prepare the people for the coming of the Messiah by proclaiming a baptism for the forgiveness of sin. John's baptism was a symbolic action in line with the symbolic actions of the prophets. The Greek word *baptisma*, from which the English word "baptism" is derived, is literally a dunking or a dipping. Water was used in rituals of purification that individuals performed on their own behalf (such as took place in the Qumran purification rituals). John's ritual of baptism was different, as Malina and Pilch note, because it was a ritual performed by someone else, not by oneself.[34] It operated as a symbol of the forgiveness of sin in preparation for the coming Messiah who was to establish Israel's theocracy.

In Ephesus, two coworkers of Paul, Aquila and Priscilla, heard Apollos speak and realized that his knowledge of the change that he was proclaiming was limited to that of the baptism of John. They instructed him "and explained the Way of God to him more accurately" (Acts 18:26). In other words, they brought him to understand that the Scriptures had been fulfilled by the agency of the God of Israel who had raised Jesus from the dead and thus constituted him as God's Messiah who would usher in an Israelite theocracy soon.

Wishing to continue his work as a traveling speaker and teacher, Apollos received a letter of recommendation from the

Jesus group of Ephesus. This recommendation in effect endorsed him as a change agent.

According to the third-generation Pauline recollections of Acts, Apollos performed two tasks when he arrived in Corinth (Acts 18:27-28). His first task supported and built up the Jesus group that Paul had already formed. Apollos worked as an eloquent speaker and teacher supporting what Paul had established. Second, he turned his attention to other Hellenized Israelites in Corinth who were not part of the Jesus group. In Corinth, he worked as a change agent using his tremendous gift of the knowledge of the Scriptures together with his rhetorical skills to bring them to accept that Jesus was God's Messiah about to usher in Israel's theocracy. They would have joined the already-existing Jesus group established by Paul in Corinth.

Finally, a comparison of the third-generation Pauline recollections that Luke provides about Apollos in Acts 18:24-28 with the authentic memory of Paul as the first generation record in 1 Corinthians 1:10–3:23 is quite revealing. Three significant parallels emerge between them:

- *Baptism is an issue raised by both accounts*: In 1 Corinthians, the divisions arise ("I belong to Paul," or "I belong to Apollos" [1:12]) because of baptism and their allegiance to those who had baptized them. In Acts 18, the matter revolves around Apollos' limited knowledge of the "baptism of John."

- *Rhetorical eloquence*: In 1 Corinthians, Paul deliberately dissociates himself from any form of "eloquent wisdom" in his preaching as it distracts from the focus on the cross of Christ. In Acts 18, Apollos is introduced as "an eloquent man." In this sense, we see a clear difference between Paul and Apollos in their rhetoric and manner of teaching.

- *Wisdom*: Paul places great importance on "spiritual wisdom" given by God's Spirit: "And we speak of these things in words not taught by human wisdom but taught by the Spirit, interpreting spiritual things to those who are spiritual" (1 Cor 2:13). Apollos is "an eloquent man" (Acts 18:24) because of his gift of rhetoric. He also speaks "with burning enthusiasm" (Acts 18:25; *zeōn tō pneumati*). The parallel with 1 Corinthians is immediately obvious in the Greek text behind the English translation. The Greek phrase *zeōn tō pneumati* translated literally reads "burning with the spirit." In both 1 Corinthians and Acts 18 the focus is on the gift of the Spirit that comes from God.

These three aspects—baptism, rhetorical eloquence, and spiritual wisdom—lie at the heart of the divisions that plagued the Jesus group of Corinth. By reading 1 Corinthians 1:10–3:23 together with Acts 18:24-28, we see that the text of Acts deepens our understanding of the dispute in Corinth and especially the reasons leading to the formation of cliques. This explains well how Apollos' eloquence, his training in wisdom, and his gift of the Spirit, would have attracted many of the Jesus group in Corinth to Apollos.

Conclusion

Our study of Apollos from the third-generation Pauline recollections in the Acts of the Apostles contributes much to our knowledge of and insight into his personality. As pointed out at the beginning of chapter 3, and as Malina has convincingly argued, the third-generation Pauline recollections were concerned with providing details regarding Paul not preserved or contained in Paul's authentic writings, the first-generation Pauline documents. Malina calls this "the principle of third-generation interest"[35] in that third-generation people in the Pauline tradition wished to preserve all the memories related to Paul.

Among the aspects that Luke fleshes out are Paul's coworkers. In our case, Luke pays attention to Apollos and his involvement with Paul. In his first letter to the Corinthians, Paul gives us a picture of Apollos that does not fill out any of the gaps. Paul is concerned with the problem of the cliques that had formed in

Corinth. He speaks of Apollos in a way that presumes everyone knows him. Writing in the third Pauline generation, Luke realizes that not many people remember those details about Apollos. He aims at filling them out and preserving Apollos' memory and his relationship with Paul.

Apollos emerges as a Hellenized Israelite from Alexandria, the cultural capital of the Hellenistic world. Our focus on Alexandria aimed at discovering what could be gleaned from its cultural and social role within the first century. Combining these insights together with Luke's recollections as the third-generation Pauline author, we attain a deeper understanding of and insight into the person of Apollos.

Apollos was well educated in the Scriptures (the Septuagint) as well as the art of rhetoric and persuasion. Apollos' Hellenistic education and his probable knowledge of Philo of Alexandria provided him with a wisdom perspective and a way of communicating the gospel of the God of Israel who raised Jesus of Nazareth from the dead. This event entailed a forthcoming Israelite theocracy. Apollos' ability and approach was different from Paul's. Some members of the Jesus group of Corinth were so enamored with Apollos' rhetorical wisdom that they embedded themselves in a clique claiming him as their leader (without his knowledge or approval). They forgot that their true embeddedness lay in the person of Christ. Paul's task was to return them to this awareness and dedication.

CONCLUSION

Apollos: Partner of Paul

wo main sources formed the basis for our study of the person of Apollos: the social and cultural world of first-century Mediterranean persons; and two New Testament documents from two Pauline generations (Paul's first letter to the Corinthians [from the first Pauline generation] and the Acts of the Apostles [from the third Pauline generation]). From these sources, Apollos emerges as a collectivistic person, a Hellenized Israelite, a change agent, an eloquent speaker. His education in Alexandria, the cultural center of the Hellenistic world, gave him a knowledge and understanding of the wisdom and philosophy of the Mediterranean world. As mentioned previously, Apollos' education in the cultural center of the Mediterranean world would be akin today to an education from a highly rated university in the United States. As a Hellenized Israelite, he "was well-versed in the scriptures" (Acts 18:24), and through the presumed influence of Philo of Alexandria he was able to use his Hellenistic education to explain his Israelite Scriptures.

In many ways, Paul and Apollos were very similar. At home in the Hellenistic world, Paul, according to Luke, was born in Tarsus, Apollos in Alexandria. Both spoke Greek, preached in

Greek, and used the Septuagint as their Sacred Scriptures. The Israelite colonies of the western Mediterranean were the loci of their activity. At home in cities, they moved from city to city as change agents proclaiming and bearing witness to the agency of God who established the resurrected Jesus as Messiah to usher in a forthcoming Israelite theocracy.

Our study has shown that there is no evidence to indicate that Apollos and Paul were rivals. As we have pointed out in chapter 3, Paul is supportive of Apollos. He presents them both as working in harmony, not in rivalry: "I planted, Apollos watered . . ." (1 Cor 3:6). Paul never speaks negatively of Apollos. Instead, his words present him more as a partner.

Their cooperative role emerges clearly from Paul's words in 1 Corinthians 4:1-13 as he moves from discussing the Corinthian cliques to addressing another issue. The inner dynamics within the Jesus group of Corinth reflect research done on small-group development. By applying these studies on small-group development to the Jesus group of Corinth, we gain a deeper understanding of that Jesus group, the cliques that emerged in this group, the role of Paul and Apollos within that Jesus group, their relationship to one another and to the cliques. For this reason, before examining 1 Corinthians 4:1-13 insofar as it reflects the cooperative role Paul and Apollos continued to play together, I shall briefly illustrate how the dynamics of small-group development apply to the foundation of the Jesus group of Corinth and its development.

Summary of the Dynamics Involved
in Small-Group Development:[1]

Stage	Relationship of Members to the Jesus Group
1. Forming	*The constitution stage of the group.* • Paul as a change agent proclaims the gospel in the *proseuchē.* • He invites the Israelites to join his Jesus group and to give loyalty to the group. • Apollos is another change agent proclaiming the same gospel. • There is a natural anxiety among the members as to whether the Jesus group will meet their needs.
2. Storming	*Jockeying for positions within the Jesus group.* • Conflicts arise: members argue against one another as well as the change agent. • Cliques are formed. • Rivalry among cliques and attempts to get others to join their cliques. • This is the stage of the Jesus group of Corinth as reflected in Paul's first letter to the Corinthians.
3. Norming	*Conflict resolution among the members of the group.* • Closer cohesion among the members of the group. • Earlier conflicts are resolved by providing a clearer understanding of their identity and the goals of the group. • This is the stage reflected by Paul's arguments, especially in the opening chapters of his first letter to the Corinthians.
4. Performing	*Members work together to accomplish the goals of the group.* • In Paul's letters there is little reference to this because it belongs to a period after his death. • It is reflected in the letters written by Paul's successors (Colossians, Ephesians, letters to Timothy and Titus).

Stage	Relationship of Members to the Jesus Group
5. Adjourning	*Members disengage from activities of the group.* • Awareness that the group is coming to an end. • In the third-generation Pauline groups there is the need to deal with the fact that with the destruction of the temple and Jerusalem the theocracy that Paul preached has not yet materialized. • Need to deal with this disappointment: the process of storming and norming begins anew.

An examination of the small Jesus group of Corinth (as reflected in Paul's first letter to the Corinthians) shows how stages 1–3 are clearly reflective of the relationship of Paul and Apollos toward the formation of the group. Stages 4 and 5 are reflective of the time after Paul and Apollos. During Paul's eighteen-month stay in Corinth (Acts 18:11), the forming stage began. Paul's efforts originated in the synagogue: "Every sabbath he would argue in the synagogue and would try to convince Jews and Greeks" (Acts 18:4). Luke indicates that Paul tried to convince Israelites (both Judeans and Hellenists) in the synagogue to form a Jesus group that would recognize God's initiative and activity in the raising of Jesus from the dead, constituting Jesus as Israel's Messiah, soon to usher in a promised Israelite theocracy. Apollos came to Corinth later and was involved as well in the forming stage of the Jesus group of Corinth. He continued Paul's work striving to bring others to join this Jesus group, as Acts 18:27-28 notes: "On his [Apollos'] arrival he greatly helped those who through grace had become believers, for he powerfully refuted the Jews in public, showing by the scriptures that the Messiah is Jesus." Paul also noted Apollos' role in this forming stage, when he said, "I planted, Apollos watered . . ." (1 Cor 3:6).

The second stage, the storming stage, is reflected in the formation of cliques within the Jesus group of Corinth established around Paul, Apollos, and Cephas. As we noted in the previous chapters, these cliques arose naturally and spontaneously within the Jesus group of Corinth. The change agents were not responsible for their creation. This storming stage is a recognized stage in the formation of small groups and one to be expected to occur within the Jesus group of Corinth.

The third stage, the norming stage, is well reflected in the opening chapters of 1 Corinthians where Paul endeavors to bring an end to these cliques. He provides the Corinthians with an understanding of their identity as a Jesus group, the relationships among themselves, and the goals they have in awaiting the resurrected Jesus' establishment of the Israelite theocracy. In this norming stage, Paul draws attention to the supportive role that Apollos has played with him as God's change agents.

First Corinthians 4:1-13 continues to reflect this norming stage: "Think of us in this way, as servants of Christ and stewards of God's mysteries" (4:1). In transitioning from the previous section dealing with ingroup conflicts to a new topic on the role of change agents, Paul implies that the Jesus-group members of Corinth should change their focus of attention from forming cliques around various change agents. Instead, Paul says, "Think of us in this way, as servants of Christ and stewards of God's mysteries" (4:1).[2]

First Corinthians 4:2-5 continues Paul's analogy introduced in 4:1 where he asked his hearers to look on himself and Apollos as "stewards" (*oikonomos*). This term refers to a "manager of a household or estate, (house) steward, manager . . . (who) manages his master's property."[3] According to Paul, the household manager was responsible to the owner of the household alone. The owner's approval was what mattered since that directed the manager's action. Paul applies this analogy in this way: he and Apollos are managers, God is the owner. For this simple reason, the Corinthians should concern themselves with their allegiance to God, not to God's managers. This is what it means to say that "I belong to Christ [God]."

Throughout this section, Paul utters no critique of Apollos; there is not the least hint of any form of rivalry between them. They are both change agents. Paul's concern is rather with bringing an end to the clique formation and reforming the group.

In drawing his arguments to a conclusion, Paul reinforces the need to turn away from the cliques. He reminds the Corinthian Jesus-group members that everything they have ultimately comes from another. In a collectivistic society, there is no such thing as a self-made man or woman. What one has comes from what one has received from family, friends, neighbors, and patrons. Ultimately, Paul intimates that all they have comes from God: "What do you have that you did not receive? And if you received it, why do you boast as if it were not a gift?" (4:7).

In a second argument (4:8-13), Paul sarcastically illustrates the worthless nature of the qualities of Apollos or Paul. The members of the Jesus group of Corinth are rich, strong, held in honor. In contrast, Paul, Apollos, and the other change agents are poor, weak, held in disrepute: "We have become like the rubbish of the world, the dregs of all things, to this very day" (4:13). They have it all; Paul and Apollos, from a human perspective, have nothing. Why then would they wish to follow them?

In this norming stage, Paul undermines the reasons for belonging to such a clique. Since he and Apollos are both change agents, and are collaborating together, there is finally no reason for the cliques to continue.

In summary, this detailed analysis of the dynamics of small-group formation as it applies to the Jesus group of Corinth is very revealing. It provides interesting insights into the relationship between Paul and Apollos. Not as rivals, but as collaborators they work in forming the Jesus group of Corinth. At the conclusion to his letter, Paul refers to their collaboration one final time: "Now concerning our brother Apollos, I strongly urged him to visit you with the other brothers, but he was not at all willing[4] to come now. He will come when he has the opportunity" (16:12). The phrase, "Now concerning" is used frequently throughout this letter. It is Paul's way of referring to topics about which the Jesus group of Corinth had written him. From what Paul says here, we presume they had written asking for Apollos to come to them. Paul is willing. As I argued previously,[5] in Paul's mind Apollos' presence would help to ensure that the disharmony arising from the cliques had ended. Once again the collaboration and harmony between Paul and Apollos is reflected here. However, Apollos declines the request and judges the situation not to be opportune. He probably feels that his presence in Corinth may cause more harm and stir up the cliques once again.

How Does Apollos Fit into Paul's Social Network?

Apollos was not recruited by Paul to join his social network as was the case with Timothy, Paul's closest associate (Acts 16:1-5). Apollos fits into Paul's social network through the actions of Priscilla and Aquila in Ephesus.

Apollos further strengthened his embeddedness within Paul's social network through the Jesus group of Corinth despite the emergence of conflicts within that group. Paul did not assign any blame to Apollos for the conflicts in this Jesus group of Corinth. Surely, this indicates that Paul understood Apollos well enough to know that he, Apollos, would not encourage actions within the Corinthian community that would have focused attention on and allegiance to himself.

Paul's references to Apollos throughout 1 Corinthians show a consistent collaboration. For Paul each provided different services for the Jesus group of Corinth. Paul was the founder, Apollos the teacher who instructed them more deeply into the message about the forthcoming Israelite theocracy. This is what Paul implies in his analogy, "I planted, Apollos watered" (3:6). At the end of the letter, Paul calls on Apollos to journey to Corinth once again to help resolve the conflicts. Seeing the situation differently from Paul, Apollos judges that his presence in Corinth would be counterproductive (16:12).

"Partners" or "collaborators" would characterize best the relationship between Paul and Apollos: they worked in harmony among the Jesus groups in preparation for the forthcoming Israelite theocracy. Apollos was embedded in the Pauline social network through his interaction with Paul's coworkers, Priscilla and Aquila, as well as with the Jesus group of Corinth that Paul had founded. But, Apollos' association with Paul and his assistants never reached the same level as Timothy shared with Paul. Timothy traveled with Paul on his numerous journeys and collaborated with him in the writing of a number of letters.

Finally, the letter to Titus, one of the Pastoral Letters, adds further evidence in support of Apollos' embeddedness in Paul's social network. This letter was written from a third-generation Pauline group to Titus, another very close companion of Paul. The conclusion of the letter mentions Apollos. The memory of this third Pauline generation reflects the same picture of Apollos as the first Pauline generation. In concluding the letter, the writer shows Paul's concern for Apollos and for his needs to be met as he leaves Crete to continue his task as change agent in spreading the message about the resurrected Jesus establishing the Israelite theocracy. "Make every effort to send Zenas the lawyer and Apollos on their way, and see that they lack nothing" (Titus 3:13). Titus shows Apollos is also viewed as embedded in Paul's social network, part of the first Pauline generation. True to the memory of the first-generation Pauline writings, this letter recalls Paul's concern for Apollos, the same concern that our first-generation sources show Paul has for those who collaborate with him.

NOTES

Introduction, pages 1–6

1. See "References to Apollos in the New Testament" (pp. xiii–xvi), which contains complete texts for all the references to Apollos. These texts are reproduced here for convenience: so that you can refer to them more easily in the course of reading this book. All Scripture quotations, unless otherwise specified, are from the New Revised Standard Version.

2. John H. Elliott, *What is Social-Scientific Criticism?* (Minneapolis: Fortress Press, 1993), 7.

3. *Random House Webster's College Dictionary* (New York: Random House, 1995), 870, s.v. "model."

4. It should be clear that I am discussing the first century *CE*. Consequently, throughout this monograph I will simply refer to the first century.

5. See pp. 46–47, and 68–69.

6. See Bruce J. Malina and John J. Pilch, "Jew and Greek/Judean and Hellenist," in *Social-Science Commentary on the Letters of Paul* (Minneapolis, MN: Fortress Press, 2006), 371–74.

Chapter 1, pages 7–19

1. See the detailed discussion of this approach in the work of A. W. H. Adkins, *From the Many to the One: A Study of Personality and Views of Human Nature in the Context of Ancient Greek Society, Values, and Beliefs* (Ithaca, NY: Cornell University Press, 1970).

2. Ibid., 3–12.

3. Grace Gredys Harris, "Concepts of Individual, Self, and Person in Description and Analysis," *American Anthropologist*, New Series 91 (Sept. 1989): 599–612.

4. See Harris's distinction between these three terms (individual, self, and person) in ibid., 600–604. The following chart is drawn up based on her careful distinctions.

5. Rom Harré, "The 'Self' as a Theoretical Concept," in *Relativism: Interpretation and Confrontation*, ed. Michael Krausz (Notre Dame, IN: University of Notre Dame Press, 1989), 387–417.

6. Ibid., 414–16.

7. Ibid., 415. Harré goes on to argue that "One who is always presented as a person, by taking over the conventions through which this social act is achieved, becomes organized as a self. That is the main empirical hypothesis which I believe to be a consequence of the considerations so far advanced, and in the testing of which the limits of the conceptual system from which it springs can be discovered."

8. Ibid., 416.

9. Homer, *The Iliad*, trans. Robert Fagles (New York, NY: Penguin Books, 1998). The lines referred to in this book are those of this translation, which differ from the standard line designations.

10. See Bruce J. Malina, *The New Testament World: Insights from Cultural Anthropology*, 3rd ed. (Louisville, KY: Westminster John Knox Press, 2001), 97–107.

11. Bruno Snell, *The Discovery of the Mind: The Greek Origins of European Thought* (New York, NY: Harper Torchbook, 1960), 1–22.

12. Ibid., 8.

13. See Plato, *The Republic*, 4.441c-442d, trans. Desmond Lee, 2nd ed. (Harmondsworth, Middlesex: Penguin Books, 1974), 218–20.

14. Charles Taylor, *Sources of the Self: The Making of the Modern Identity* (Cambridge, MA: Harvard University Press, 1989), 117.

15. This phrase is taken from Bruce J. Malina and Jerome H. Neyrey, "First Century Personality: Dyadic, not Individual," in *The Social World of Luke-Acts: Models for Interpretation*, ed. Jerome H. Neyrey (Peabody, MA: Hendrickson Publishers, 1991), 74.

Chapter 2, pages 20–45

1. I base myself here largely on the work of Harry C. Triandis. Among his numerous publications, the following have been the most helpful in this study, "Cross-Cultural Studies of Individualism and Collectivism," in *Cross-Cultural Perspectives, Nebraska Symposium on Motivation, 1989*, ed. John J. Berman, vol. 37 (Lincoln, NE: University of Nebraska Press, 1990), 41–133;

Culture and Social Behavior (New York, NY: McGraw-Hill, 1994); *Individualism and Collectivism* (Boulder, CO: Westview Press, 1995).

2. Triandis, *Culture and Social Behavior*, 22.

3. Ibid.

4. Peter L. Berger and Thomas Luckmann (*The Social Construction of Reality: A Treatise in the Sociology of Knowledge* [Garden City, NY: Doubleday, 1966], 120) insightfully define socialization in this way: "Socialization which may be defined as the comprehensive and consistent induction of an individual into the objective world of a society or a sector of it." We have already discussed another dimension of this socialization in the previous chapter when we discussed the concept of psychological symbiosis.

5. This chart is a summary of the discussion found in Triandis, *Individualism and Collectivism*, 71–79. I am also indebted to him for his explanation of how these attributes work themselves out in an individualistic or a collectivistic culture.

6. These are terms that Triandis has borrowed from the work of S. H. Schwartz, "Beyond Individualism and Collectivism: New Cultural Dimensions of Values," in *Individualism and Collectivism: Theory, Method, and Applications*, eds. U. Kim, H. C. Triandis, C. Kagitcibasi, S-C. Choi, and G. Yoon (Newbury Park, CA: Sage, 1994), 85–122.

7. The Japanese scholar D. Matsumoto has shown from his studies on Japanese society (which is a collectivistic society) that they experience sadness more frequently than happiness. American culture, as an individualistic culture, experiences the reverse: happiness more often than sadness. (See D. Matsumoto, "Cultural Differences in the Perception of Emotion," *Journal of Cross-Cultural Psychology* 20 [1989]: 92–105. See also "Cultural Influences on Facial Expressions of Emotions," *Southern Journal of Communication* 56 [1991], 128–37.)

8. This phrase is taken from Bruce J. Malina and Jerome H. Neyrey, "First Century Personality: Dyadic, not Individual," in *The Social World of Luke-Acts: Models for Interpretation*, ed. Jerome H. Neyrey (Peabody, MA: Hendrickson Publishers, 1991), 74.

9. Bruce Malina, "The Individual and the Community—Personality in the Social World of Early Christianity," *BTB* 9 (1979): 127.

10. John J. Pilch and Bruce J. Malina, eds., *Handbook of Biblical Social Values* (Peabody, MA: Hendrickson Publishers, 2000), 55; s.v. "dyadism."

11. Bruce J. Malina and Jerome H. Neyrey, *Portraits of Paul: An Archaeology of Ancient Personality* (Louisville, KY: Westminster John Knox Press, 1996), 158.

12. Edward T. Hall, *The Silent Language* (Greenwich, CT: Fawcett Publications, 1966), 112.

13. See Simon Hornblower and Antony Spawforth, eds., *Oxford Classical Dictionary*, 3rd ed. (Oxford: Oxford University Press, 2003), 362; s.v. "collegium."

14. W. E. Nunnally, "Gamaliel," in David Noel Freedman, ed., *Eerdmans Dictionary of the Bible* (Grand Rapids, MI: William B. Eerdmans Publishing Company, 2000), 481.

15. Malina and Neyrey, *Portraits of Paul*, 161.

16. For an excellent and insightful explanation of circumcision within the framework of the first-century Israelite world (both within and outside of the land of Israel), see Bruce J. Malina, *Timothy: Paul's Closest Associate*, Paul's Social Network: Brothers and Sisters in Faith (Collegeville, MN: Liturgical Press, 2008), 102–5.

17. Bruce J. Malina and John J. Pilch, *Social-Science Commentary on the Book of Acts* (Minneapolis, MN: Fortress Press, 2008), 106.

18. Frederick William Danker, ed., *A Greek-English Lexicon of the New Testament and Other Early Christian Literature*, 3rd ed. (Chicago, IL: University of Chicago Press, 2000), 818; s.v. *"pistis."*

19. Ibid.

20. I follow here the work of Malina and Neyrey, *Portraits of Paul*, 188–98. In examining the values of the first-century Mediterranean world, Malina and Neyrey draw upon a model first introduced by the anthropologists F. R. Kluckhohn and F. L. Strodtbeck (*Variations in Value Orientation* [New York, NY: Harper & Row, 1961]) and further developed by John Papajohn and John Spiegel (*Transactions in Families* [San Francisco, CA: Jossey-Bass, 1975]) in order to identify the variations in values that occur among different ethnic groups. What is foundational in this study is the importance that is given to the value of being. This value arises from the understanding that collectivistic persons have of their world and their place within it.

Chapter 3, pages 46–67

1. Bruce J. Malina, *Timothy: Paul's Closest Associate*, Paul's Social Network: Brothers and Sisters in Faith (Collegeville, MN: Liturgical Press, 2008).

2. *Random House Webster's College Dictionary* (New York, NY: Random House, 1995), 555; s.v. "generation."

3. Malina, *Timothy: Paul's Closest Associate*, 47.

4. Ibid., 44.

5. Webster's Dictionary defines "agonistic" as: "1. combative; striving to overcome in argument; 2. straining for effect; 3. of or pertaining to ancient

Greek athletic contests; 4. pertaining to a behavioral response to an aggressive encounter, as attack or appeasement" (*Random House Webster's College Dictionary*, 27).

6. Bruce J. Malina and John J. Pilch, *Social Science Commentary on the Letters of Paul* (Minneapolis, MN: Fortress Press, 2006), 368.

7. John J. Pilch, *The Cultural Dictionary of the Bible* (Collegeville, MN: Liturgical Press, 1999), 5.

8. Malina and Pilch, *Social Science Commentary on the Letters of Paul*, 342. In the previous chapter we discussed different groups in which Apollos was embedded. Cliques were not treated there because Apollos was not embedded in these Corinthian cliques. Instead, people formed a clique around his name.

9. See *Random House Webster's College Dictionary*, 255, s.v. "clique."

10. Malina and Pilch, *Social Science Commentary on the Letters of Paul*, 63.

11. Ibid., 331.

12. Pilch, *The Cultural Dictionary of the Bible*, 81–82.

13. Malina and Pilch, *Social Science Commentary on the Letters of Paul*, 335–37.

14. Bruce Malina and Jerome H. Neyrey, *Portraits of Paul: An Archaeology of Ancient Personality* (Louisville, KY: Westminster John Knox Press, 1996), 199.

15. Henry George Liddell and Robert Scott, *Greek English Lexicon With a Revised Supplement* (Oxford: Clarendon Press, 1996), 358–59; s.v. "*grammateus*."

16. Frederick William Danker, ed., *A Greek-English Lexicon of the New Testament and Other Early Christian Literature*, 3rd ed. (Chicago, IL: University of Chicago Press, 2000), 954; s.v. "*suzētēsis*."

17. Malina and Pilch, *Social-Science Commentary on the Letters of Paul*, 131.

18. Ibid.

19. Ben Witherington III, *Conflict and Community in Corinth: A Socio-Rhetorical Commentary on 1 and 2 Corinthians* (Grand Rapids, MI: Eerdmans Publishing Co., 1995), 317.

20. Ibid.

Chapter 4, pages 68–101

1. The word Diaspora is defined in this way, "(1) **state or condition of being scattered,** *dispersion* of those who are dispersed (Is 49:6, Ps 146:2; 2

Macc 1:27; PsSol 8:28) . . . (2) **the place in which the dispersed are found,**
dispersion, diaspora (Jdth 5:19; TestAsh 7:2)." (Frederick William Danker, ed.,
A Greek-English Lexicon of the New Testament and other Early Christian Litera-
ture, 3rd ed. [Chicago, IL: University of Chicago Press, 2000], 236).

2. Webster's Dictionary defines Diaspora in this way, "1. the scattering
of the Jews to countries outside of Palestine after the Babylonian captivity.
2. . . . the body of Jews living in countries outside Palestine or modern
Israel. 3. . . . such countries collectively. 4. . . . any group migration or
flight from a country or region; dispersion. 5. . . . any group that has been
dispersed outside its traditional homeland" (*Random House Webster's College
Dictionary* [New York, NY: Random House, 1990], 373).

3. See John J. Pilch, *Stephen: Paul and the Hellenist Israelites.* Paul's Social
Network: Brothers and Sisters in Faith (Collegeville, MN: Liturgical Press,
2008), 4–7. It is interesting to note in the quotation from Webster's Dictionary in the previous note how the idea of Diaspora as tied to the concept
of a forced removal is still predominant. For this very reason, Pilch's sug-
gestion to use the term "colonies" instead is really significant.

4. Arye Edrei and Doron Mendels, "A Split Jewish Diaspora: Its Dramatic
Consequences," *Journal for the Study of the Pseudepigrapha* 16, no. 2 (2007):
91–137.

5. Ibid., 92.

6. This chart is compiled from ibid, 91–137.

7. Edrei and Mendels adopt more of an intermediary position for Alexandria and Egypt: "If we were to draw up a scale depicting the gap between
the communities, with the eastern diaspora in white and the western
diaspora in black, Egypt would probably be depicted in gray" (112, n. 36).
I do not think that the examples they cite clearly demonstrate this intermediary position. From my text, the closeness of Alexandria and Egypt to the
colonies of the western Mediterranean emerges more convincingly.

8. See an excellent map of Alexandria in Judith McKenzie "Glimpsing
Alexandria from Archaeological Evidence," *Journal of Roman Archaeology* 16
(2003): 35–61, esp. 42–43.

9. Erich S. Gruen, "The Jews in Alexandria," in *Diaspora: Jews amidst
Greeks and Romans* (Cambridge, MA: Harvard University Press, 2002),
54–83.

10. Ibid., 83.

11. In this section, I follow closely the formidable research presented by
Lee I. Levine (professor in Jewish history and archaeology at the Hebrew
University) in his 748-page study *The Ancient Synagogue: The First Thousand
Years* (New Haven, CT: Yale University Press, 2000), esp. chaps. 1–5, pp.
1–159. In this treatment I focus especially on the Western Diaspora and

Alexandria in particular. I use the transliteration *proseuchē* for "the place of prayer."

12. See definitions of *proseuchē* in Danker, *A Greek-English Lexicon of the New Testament and other Early Christian Literature*, 879; and Henry George Liddell and Robert Scott, *Greek-English Lexicon With a Revised Supplement* (Oxford: Clarendon Press, 1996), 1511.

13. The epigraphical evidence has been collected and analyzed by William Horbury and David Noy, *Jewish Inscriptions of Graeco-Roman Egypt: With an Index of the Jewish Inscriptions of Egypt and Cyrenaica* (Cambridge: Cambridge University Press, 1992).

14. Ibid., 35 (no. 22).

15. Ibid., 42 (no. 25).

16. P. M. Fraser, *Ptolemaic Alexandria*. vol. 1 (Oxford: Clarendon Press, 1972), 190.

17. Ibid.

18. Horbury and Noy, *Jewish Inscriptions*, 212 (no. 125).

19. See Günter Mayer, *Index Philoneus* (Berlin: W. de Gruyter, 1974), 247.

20. For example, Philo writes in his work, *Flaccus*, 48 "if they were deprived of their *houses of prayers*, would at the same time be deprived of all means of showing their *piety* towards their benefactors . . . they would no longer have any *sacred places* in which they could declare their gratitude" (in C. D. Yonge, trans., *The Works of Philo: Complete and Unabridged* [Peabody, MA: Hendrickson Publishers, 1993], 729; emphasis added).

21. For example, Philo writes in his work, *Embassy*, 312: "These assemblies were . . . schools of temperance and justice, as the men who met in them were studiers of virtue" (in ibid., 785).

22. See, Philo, *Embassy*, 133 (in ibid., 769).

23. See Levine, *The Ancient Synagogue*, 55.

24. Ibid., 31–41, 72–73.

25. Ibid., 155.

26. D. F. Watson, "Education: Jewish and Greco-Roman," in *Dictionary of New Testament Background*, eds. Craig A. Evans and Stanley E. Porter (Downers Grove, IL: InterVarsity Press, 2000), 312.

27. Vernon K. Robbins, "Chreia and Pronouncement Story in Synoptic Studies," in *Patterns of Persuasion in the Gospels*, eds. Vernon K. Robbins and Burton L. Mack (Sonoma, CA: Polebridge Press, 1989) 1–30.

28. Bruce J. Malina and Jerome H. Neyrey, *Portraits of Paul: An Archaeology of Ancient Personality* (Louisville, KY: Westminster John Knox Press, 1996), 4.

29. Burton L. Mack, "Elaboration of the Chreia in the Hellenistic School," in *Patterns of Persuasion in the Gospels*, 33.

30. For a more detailed examination of the "perfect argument" and its practical application see Patrick J. Hartin, *James*, Sacra Pagina, vol. 14 (Collegeville, MN: Liturgical Press, 2003), 124–39.

31. John J. Pilch and Bruce J. Malina, eds., *Handbook of Biblical Social Values* (Peabody, MA: Hendrickson Publishers, 2000), 115; s.v. "hospitality."

32. Ibid., 115–18.

33. There is an interesting monograph on the theme of hospitality in *The Odyssey*: Steve Reece, *The Stranger's Welcome: Oral Theory and the Aesthetics of the Homeric Hospitality Scene* (Ann Arbor, MI: University of Michigan Press, 1993).

34. Bruce J. Malina and John J. Pilch, *Social-Science Commentary on the Letters of Paul* (Minneapolis, MN: Fortress Press, 2006), 333.

35. Bruce J. Malina, *Timothy: Paul's Closest Associate*, Paul's Social Network: Brothers and Sisters in Faith (Collegeville, MN: Liturgical Press, 2008), 44.

Conclusion, pages 102–109

1. This chart is developed from the research presented by B. W. Tuckman, "Developmental Sequence in Small Groups," *Psychological Bulletin* 63 (1965): 384–99. This research was substantiated and given more precision in the work of Richard L. Moreland and John M. Levine, "Group Dynamics Over Time: Development and Socialization in Small Groups," in *The Social Psychology of Time: New Perspectives*, ed. Joseph E. McGrath (Newbury Park, CA: Sage, 1988), 151–81. Bruce J. Malina has used these studies in a masterful way in adapting and applying them to studies of small groups in the world of the New Testament. There is an excellent summary of his perspectives (to which I am gratefully indebted in my summary provided here) in "Small-Group Development,", in *Social-Science Commentary on the Letters of Paul*, eds. Bruce J. Malina and John J. Pilch (Minneapolis, MN: Fortress Press, 2006), 397–400.

2. See Malina and Pilch, *Social-Science Commentary on the Letters of Paul*, 75.

3. Frederick William Danker, ed., *A Greek-English Lexicon of the New Testament and Other Early Christian Literature*, 3rd ed. (Chicago, IL: University of Chicago Press, 2000), 698; s.v. *"oikonomos."*

4. Other texts read: "It was not at all God's will for him to come now." God's agency is clearly acknowledged here. The fact that Apollos was unwilling is ultimately seen to reflect the will of God.

5. See pp. 54–67.

BIBLIOGRAPHY

Adkins, A. W. H. *From the Many to the One: A Study of Personality and Views of Human Nature in the Context of Ancient Greek Society, Values, and Beliefs*. Ithaca, NY: Cornell University Press, 1970.

Bagnall, Roger S., and Dominic W. Rathbone, eds. *Egypt from Alexander to the Early Christians: An Archaeological and Historical Guide*. Los Angeles, CA: J. Paul Getty Museum, 2004.

Barclay, John M. G. *Jews in the Mediterranean Diaspora: From Alexander to Trajan (323 B.C.E.–111 C.E.)*. Berkeley/Los Angeles, CA: University of California Press, 1996.

Berger, Peter L., and Thomas Luckmann. *The Social Construction of Reality: A Treatise in the Sociology of Knowledge*. Garden City, NY: Doubleday, 1966.

Bingen, Jean. *Hellenistic Egypt: Monarchy, Society, Economy, Culture*. Edited by Roger S. Bagnall. Berkeley/Los Angeles, CA: University of California Press, 2007.

Cohen, Shaye J. D. *The Beginnings of Jewishness: Boundaries, Varieties, Uncertainties*. Berkeley/Los Angeles, CA: University of California Press, 1999.

Collins, Raymond. *First Corinthians*. Sacra Pagina. Vol. 7. Collegeville, MN: Liturgical Press, 1999.

Cribiore, Raffaella. *Gymnastics of the Mind: Greek Education in Hellenistic and Roman Egypt*. Princeton, NJ: Princeton University Press, 2001.

Danker, Frederick William, ed. *A Greek-English Lexicon of the New Testament and Other Early Christian Literature*. 3rd ed. Chicago, IL: University of Chicago Press, 2000. Revised based on Walter Bauer's *Griechisch-deutsches Wörterbuch zu den Schriften des Neuen Testaments und der Frühchristlichen Literatur*, 6th ed., edited by Kurt Aland and Barbara Aland with Viktor Reichmann, and on previous English editions by W. F. Arndt, F. W. Gringrich, and F. W. Danker.

Edrei, Arye, and Doron Mendels. "A Split Jewish Diaspora: Its Dramatic Consequences." *Journal for the Study of the Pseudepigrapha* 16, no. 2 (2007): 91–137.

Elliott, John H. *What is Social-Scientific Criticism?* Minneapolis, MN: Fortress Press, 1993.

Evans, Craig A., and Stanley E. Porter, eds. *Dictionary of New Testament Background.* Downers Grove, IL: InterVarsity Press, 2000.

Foster, George M. "The Dyadic Contract: A Model for the Social Structure of a Mexican Peasant Village." *American Anthropologist.* New Series 63, no. 6 (1961): 1173–92.

Fraser, P. M. *Ptolemaic Alexandria.* Vol. I, Text. Vol. II, Notes. Vol. III, Indexes. Oxford: Clarendon Press, 1972.

Freedman, David Noel, ed. *Eerdmans Dictionary of the Bible.* Grand Rapids, MI: William B. Eerdmans Publishing Company, 2000.

Geertz, Clifford. "From the Native's Point of View: On the Nature of Anthropological Understanding." In *Meaning in Anthropology*, edited by Keith H. Basso and Henry A. Selby. Albuquerque, NM: University of New Mexico Press, 1976.

Gruen, Erich S. "The Jews in Alexandria." Chap. 2 (54–83) in *Diaspora: Jews amidst Greeks and Romans.* Cambridge, MA: Harvard University Press, 2002.

Hall, Edward T. *The Silent Language.* Greenwich, CT: Fawcett Publications, 1966.

Harré, Rom. "The 'Self' as a Theoretical Concept." In *Relativism: Interpretation and Confrontation*, edited by Michael Krausz, 387–417. Notre Dame, IN: University of Notre Dame Press, 1989.

Harris, Grace Gredys. "Concepts of Individual, Self, and Person in Description and Analysis." *American Anthropologist.* New Series 91 (Sept. 1989): 599–612.

Hartin, Patrick J. *James.* Sacra Pagina. Vol. 14. Collegeville, MN: Liturgical Press, 2003.

Hartog, François, *Memories of Odysseus: Frontier Tales from Ancient Greece.* Translated by Janet Lloyd. Chicago, IL: University of Chicago Press, 2001.

Horbury, William, and David Noy. *Jewish Inscriptions of Graeco-Roman Egypt: With an Index of the Jewish Inscriptions of Egypt and Cyrenaica.* Cambridge: Cambridge University Press, 1992.

Hornblower, Simon, and Antony Spawforth, eds. *Oxford Classical Dictionary*. 3rd ed. Oxford: Oxford University Press, 2003.

Kluckhohn, F. R., and F. L. Strodtbeck. *Variations in Value Orientation*. New York: Harper & Row, 1961.

Levine, Lee I. *The Ancient Synagogue: The First Thousand Years*. New Haven, CT: Yale University Press, 2000.

Liddell, Henry George, and Robert Scott. *Greek-English Lexicon with a Revised Supplement*. Oxford: Clarendon Press, 1996.

Mack, Burton L. "Elaboration of the Chreia in the Hellenistic School." In Mack and Robbins, *Patterns of Persuasion in the Gospels*, 31–67.

Mack, Burton L., and Vernon K. Robbins. *Patterns of Persuasion in the Gospels*. Sonoma, CA: Polebridge Press, 1989.

Malina, Bruce J. *Christian Origins and Cultural Anthropology: Practical Models for Biblical Interpretation*. Atlanta, GA: John Knox Press, 1986.

———. "Dealing with Biblical (Mediterranean) Characters: A Guide for U.S. Consumers." *BTB* 19 (1989): 127–41.

———. "The Individual and the Community—Personality in the Social World of Early Christianity." *BTB* 9 (1979): 126–38.

———. *The New Testament World: Insights from Cultural Anthropology*. 3rd ed. Louisville, KY: Westminster John Knox Press, 2001.

———. "The Social World Implied in the Letters of the Christian Bishop-Martyr (Named Ignatius of Antioch)." In *Society of Biblical Literature Seminar Papers*, 71–119. Vol. 2. Missoula, MT: Scholars Press, 1978.

———. *Timothy: Paul's Closest Associate*. Paul's Social Network: Brothers and Sisters in Faith. Collegeville, MN: Liturgical Press, 2008.

Malina, Bruce J., and Jerome H. Neyrey. "First Century Personality: Dyadic, not Individual." In *The Social World of Luke-Acts: Models for Interpretation*, edited by Jerome H. Neyrey, 67–96. Peabody, MA: Hendrickson Publishers, 1991.

———. *Portraits of Paul: An Archaeology of Ancient Personality*. Louisville, KY: Westminster John Knox Press, 1996.

Malina, Bruce J., and John J. Pilch. *Social-Science Commentary on the Book of Acts*. Minneapolis, MN: Fortress Press, 2008.

———. *Social-Science Commentary on the Letters of Paul*. Minneapolis, MN: Fortress Press, 2006.

Matsumoto, D. "Cultural Differences in the Perception of Emotion." *Journal of Cross-Cultural Psychology* 20 (1989): 92–105.

————. "Cultural Influences on Facial Expressions of Emotions." *Southern Journal of Communication* 56 (1991): 128–37.

Mayer, Günter. *Index Philoneus*. Berlin: W. de Gruyter, 1974.

McKenzie, Judith. "Glimpsing Alexandria from Archaeological Evidence." *Journal of Roman Archaeology* 16 (2003): 35–61.

Moreland, Richard L., and John M. Levine. "Group Dynamics Over Time: Development and Socialization in Small Groups." In *The Social Psychology of Time: New Perspectives*, edited by Joseph E. McGrath. Newbury Park, CA: Sage, 1988.

Neyrey, Jerome H. *Paul in Other Words: A Cultural Reading of His Letters*. Louisville, KY: Westminster John Knox Press, 1990.

————, ed. *The Social World of Luke-Acts: Models for Interpretation*. Peabody, MA: Hendrickson Publishers, 1991.

Nunnally, W. E. "Gamaliel." In Freedman, *Eerdmans Dictionary of the Bible*, 181-82.

Papajohn, John, and John Spiegel. *Transactions in Families*. San Francisco, CA: Jossey-Bass, 1975.

Pilch, John J. *The Cultural Dictionary of the Bible*. Collegeville, MN: Liturgical Press, 1999.

————. *Stephen: Paul and the Hellenist Israelites*. Paul's Social Network: Brothers and Sisters in Faith. Collegeville, MN: Liturgical Press, 2008.

Pilch, John J., and Bruce J. Malina, eds. *Handbook of Biblical Social Values*. Peabody, MA: Hendrickson Publishers, 2000.

Reece, Steve. *The Stranger's Welcome: Oral Theory and the Aesthetics of the Homeric Hospitality Scene*. Ann Arbor, MI: University of Michigan Press, 1993.

Robbins, Vernon K. "Chreia and Pronouncement Story in Synoptic Studies." In Mack and Robbins, *Patterns of Persuasion in the Gospels*, 1–30.

Schenck, Kenneth. *A Brief Guide to Philo*. Louisville, KY: Westminster John Knox Press, 2005.

Scholer, David M., ed. "Foreword: An Introduction to Philo." In *The Works of Philo: Complete and Unabridged*, translated by C. D. Yonge. Peabody, MA: Hendrickson Publishers, 1993.

Schwartz, S. H. "Beyond Individualism and Collectivism: New Cultural Dimensions of Values." In *Individualism and Collectivism: Theory, Method, and Applications*, edited by U. Kim, H. C. Triandis, C. Kagitcibasi, S-C. Choi, and G. Yoon. Newbury Park, CA: Sage, 1994.

Snell, Bruno. *The Discovery of the Mind: The Greek Origins of European Thought.* New York, NY: Harper Torchbook, 1960.

Taylor, Charles. *Sources of the Self: The Making of the Modern Identity.* Cambridge, MA: Harvard University Press, 1989.

Tichy, Noel. "An Analysis of Clique Formation and Structure in Organizations." *Administrative Science Quarterly* 18, no. 2 (1973): 194–208.

Triandis. Harry C. "Cross-Cultural Studies of Individualism and Collectivism." In *Cross-Cultural Perspectives, Nebraska Symposium on Motivation, 1989,* edited by John J. Berman, 41–133. Vol. 37. Lincoln, NE: University of Nebraska Press, 1990.

———. *Culture and Social Behavior.* New York, NY: McGraw-Hill, 1994.

———. *Individualism and Collectivism.* Boulder, CO: Westview Press, 1995.

Tuckman, B.W. "Developmental Sequence in Small Groups." *Psychological Bulletin* 63 (1965): 384–99.

Witherington III, Ben. *Conflict and Community in Corinth: A Socio-Rhetorical Commentary on 1 and 2 Corinthians.* Grand Rapids, MI: William B. Eerdmans Publishing Company, 1995.

ANCIENT TEXTS

Dio Cocceianus, Chrysostomus. *Dio Chrysostom.* Translated by J. W. Cohoon. Vol. 1. Cambridge, MA: Harvard University Press, 1949.

———. *Dio Chrysostom.* Translated by H. Lamar Crosby. Vol. 4. Cambridge, MA: Harvard University Press, 1956.

Homer. *The Iliad.* Translated by Robert Fagles. New York: Penguin Books, 1998.

———. *Iliad: Books 1–12.* Translated by A.T. Murray. Revised by William F. Wyatt. Cambridge, MA: Harvard University Press, 1999.

Josephus, Flavius. *The Life and Against Apion.* Vol 1. Edited and translated by H. St. J. Thackery. Cambridge, MA: Harvard University Press, 1961.

———. *Jewish Antiquities, Books XV–XVII.* Vol. 8. Cambridge, MA: Harvard University Press, 1963.

Philo. "On the Embassy to Gaius." In *The Works of Philo: Complete and Unabridged,* translated by C. D. Yonge. Peabody, MA: Hendrickson Publishers, 1993, 756–90.

———. "Flaccus." In ibid., 725–41.

Philostratus and Eunapius: *The Lives of the Sophists.* Translated by William Cave Wright. Cambridge, MA: Cambridge University Press, 1961.

Plato. *The Republic.* Translated by Desmond Lee. 2nd ed. Harmondsworth, Middlesex: Penguin Books, 1974.

Shutt, R. J. H., trans. *Letter of Aristeas.* In *The Old Testament Pseudepigrapha*, edited by James H. Charlesworth, 7–34. Vol. 2. London: Darton, Longman & Todd, 1985.

Strabo. *The Geography of Strabo.* Vol. 6. Translated by Horace Leonard Jones. Cambridge, MA: Harvard University Press, 1960.

INDEX OF PERSONS AND SUBJECTS

Abraham, 58
Achaeans, 14
Achaia, 96
Achilles, 13–14, 33, 91
Acts of the Apostles, xvi, 1, 3–4,
  35, 42, 45–46, 48–50, 57, 62,
  67–68, 75, 78, 94, 100, 102
adelphoi, 40
Adjourning, 105
Adkins, A. W. H., 9, 13, 17, 110, 118
Aegean Sea, 96
Africans, 13
Agamemnon, 13–14
agathos, 9
agonistic, 50, 51, 113
  agonistic culture, 49
Ajax, 16
Alexander the Great, 13, 33, 76, 78
Alexandria, xvi, 3–4, 19, 25, 27,
  31–32, 35–37, 44, 54, 68–69,
  71–95, 98, 101–2, 115–16, 119,
  121
  Alexandrian Israelites, 83
  cultic institutions, 77
  cultural world, 45, 49, 56, 75,
    90, 92, 94, 102
  Great Library, 77–78, 91
  Museum, 77, 91, 118
  native of, 19, 31, 35, 44, 75,
    90–91
  Ptolemaic Alexandria, 80, 116,
    119
Alexandria ad Aegyptum, 76

allegory, 83
alternate state of consciousness,
  54–57
anachronism, 7, 97
anachronistic fallacy, 84–85
Anatolia, 78
  Anatolian highway system,
    96
ancient Mediterranean society, 9,
  15, 29
Andromache, 24
Antioch, 66, 71, 120
  Antioch of Pisidia, 95
Apion, 39, 79, 122
Apocrypha, 72, 74
Apollos, xii, xvi, 1–5, 7–8, 17–20,
  22, 24–29, 31–32, 34–49, 52–54,
  57–59, 62–69, 75–85, 90–96,
  98–110, 114, 117
  Apollos in Alexandria, 80, 94,
    102
  Apollos' identity, 4, 17, 24, 31
  Apollos: Partner of Paul, 5,
    102
  Apollos' sense of self, 8, 17–20
Apollos group, 28
apostle, 42, 57
  apostleship, 43
Arabia and the East, 77
  Arab world, 29–30
  Arabian Desert, 55
archaeological evidence, 4, 87,
  94, 115, 121

Aristotle, 33, 92
Asclepius, 33
Asia Minor, 70, 71, 85, 94
    Province of Asia, 95
assemblies, 116
associations, 32, 33
Assyrians, 70
astronomy, 78
asulon, 86
Athens, 60, 63, 76, 78
attitudes, 22, 23, 25, 26, 37, 44, 46
Attributions, 23, 24
Augustus, 95
authentic memory, 99

Babylonia, 71
    Babylonians, 70
    Babylonian Talmud, 5
baptism, xvi, 34, 52, 53, 96,
    98–100
    baptisma, 98
    baptism of John, xvi, 96,
        98–99
    baptism for the forgiveness
        of sin, 98
Barnabas, 48
behavior, 2, 6, 21–23, 27–29, 61,
    112, 122
Berenice, 85
Berger, Peter L., 112, 118
Beta, 76
biologistic, 9–10
boot, 8
Booths (Sukkoth), 88
Briseis, 13–14
brothers and sisters, xiii, xiv, xxv,
    35–36, 40, 43, 113, 115, 117,
    120–21
"burning with the spirit," 100

Caesarea, 87
Callimachus, 78

Capernaum, 87
capital, 76, 95, 101
car, 8
Cephas, xiii, xiv, 40, 49, 52–53,
    58–59, 66, 105
Chalcedon, 6
change agent, 25, 42, 52, 54,
    56–58, 60–62, 68–69, 75, 94,
    98–99, 102–7, 109
    God's change agents, 106
Chiron, 33
Chreia and Pronouncement
    Story, 116, 121
Cicero, 92
circumcision, 35, 113
city, 3, 6, 17, 31 32, 35 36, 57,
    59–60, 66, 69–72, 75–76, 78–80,
    83, 87–88, 91, 95, 103, 112
    city gate, 88
Cleopatra, 85
clique, 26, 27, 40, 49, 51–54,
    59–62, 64–66, 69, 100–101,
    103–8, 114, 122
    cliquer, 51
    formation of cliques, 59–60,
        100, 105
coalition, 51
Codex Alexandrinus, 82
Codex Vaticanus, 82
Cognitions, 23, 24
collectivist, 20, 22, 24, 26–28, 31,
    36, 37, 44, 46
    collectivistic culture, 4, 20, 22,
        23, 28, 37, 41, 44, 46, 52, 112
        embedded in, vii, 4, 20
    collectivist self, 20
    collectivism, 20, 111–12, 121–22
collegia, 32
colonies, 36, 70–75, 79, 83–85,
    87–90, 103, 115
    eastern colonies, 72–74
    western colonies, 36, 72–74

communal worship, 88, 90
communication, 72, 112, 121
community, xvi, 1, 14, 20, 27,
    31–33, 39, 48, 50–52, 63–64, 69,
    73, 79–80, 83, 85, 86, 88, 90–92,
    94, 97, 108, 112, 114, 120, 122
  Corinthian community, 1, 48,
    52, 63–64, 108
  Hellenized Israelite
    community, 4, 32, 69, 79–80,
    83, 85–86, 90–92, 94
conflict, 4, 23, 26–27, 49, 50, 54,
    57, 80, 98, 104, 114, 122
  conflict resolution, 23, 26, 104
conformity, 10–12, 74, 93
conscience, 37
"Construction Site," 76
Corinth, vii, 3–5, 18, 24–27, 35–37,
    40, 45–46, 49, 51–54, 57–60,
    62–66, 68–70, 83, 98, 99, 100–109
  Jesus group of Corinth, 5,
    26–27, 36–37, 40, 45, 49,
    51–54, 57–60, 62–63, 83,
    100–109
  Corinth and Apollos, 25,
    35–36, 98
  Corinthian conflict, 26
Crete, 109
culture, vii, ix, 4–5, 7–10, 13, 14,
    17, 20–23, 28, 30, 36–37, 41, 44,
    46, 49–52, 55, 60, 75, 78, 80, 83,
    91, 112, 118, 122
  cultural world, 45, 49, 56, 75,
    90, 92, 94, 102
  agonistic culture, 64
  collectivistic culture, 4, 20,
    22–23, 28, 37, 41, 44, 46, 52,
    112
  individualistic culture, 17, 22,
    23, 112

Damascus, 42, 54

Damascus Document, 87
Danker, Frederick William, 113–19
De Inventione, 92
De Optimo Genere Oratorum, 92
De Oratore, 92
De Partitione Oratoriae, 92
dedicatory inscriptions, 85
dedicatory plaques, 85–86
deliberative, 93
Delta, 76
desire, 16, 27, 80
Diaspora, 35, 69, 70–71, 114–15,
    118–19
  eastern diaspora, 71, 115
  western diaspora, 35, 69, 71,
    115
dietary laws, 35
Dio Chrysostom, 60–61, 122
Diogenes, 60
disciple, 33–34, 61
dispersion, 69, 114–15
Doolittle, Eliza, 12
Dor, 87
dyad, 52
  dyadic, 28, 52–53, 111–12,
    119–20
  dyadism, 28, 112

ecology, 21
Edrei, Arye, 71, 115, 119
education, 4, 19, 31, 36–38, 43–44,
    90–94, 101–2, 116, 118
  education system, 91
Egypt, 32, 70, 72, 74, 76–77, 79,
    84–85, 87–89, 91, 115–16,
    118–19
  Egyptians, 32, 76, 80
elite, 31, 70, 75, 92
Elliott, John H., 2, 110, 119
eloquence, 61–62, 66, 99, 100
  eloquent man, xvi, 19, 62, 75,
    77, 90–92, 94, 99

eloquent speaker, 99, 102
eloquent wisdom, xiii, 63, 99
embedded, 4, 17, 18–21, 23–39,
    41–46, 51, 58, 69, 75, 80, 90–91,
    101, 108–9, 114
    embeddedness, 35–37, 49, 52,
        101, 108–9
    embedded group, 39
emotions, 11, 23, 24, 112, 121
emperor, 86–87, 95
endurance, 41–42
Ephesus, xvi, 19, 25, 27, 34–35,
    37, 43, 69, 84, 90, 94–99, 108
epideictic, 93
epigraphical evidence, 85, 116
    epigraphical material, 85
ethnicity, 36
    ethnic group, 17, 25, 27, 29,
        31–32, 44, 80, 90
    ethnic identity, 79, 84
ethnocentric fallacy, 7–8, 44
ētor, 15

faction, 51, 65
faith, 3, 33–34, 37–39, 43, 55, 58,
    68, 91, 113, 115, 117, 120–21
    faithfulness, 37–41
fame, 14–15
family, 11, 17, 23, 29, 30–34, 51,
    85, 97, 107
    family and friends, 97
fictive, 29, 32–33, 40, 97
    fictive birth, 29
    fictive brother(s and sisters), 40
    fictive kinship, 32, 35–36, 52, 66
        fictive kinship group, 27,
            29, 32–33, 38, 40, 42
    fictive siblings, 32
foreigners, 97
forming, 104, 107
    forming stage, 105
fragmentation, 15–16

Fraser, P. M., 86, 116, 119

Gamaliel, 33–34, 113, 121
generation, 47, 58, 88, 113
    first generation (Pauline), vii,
        4, 46–49, 57, 99, 100, 109
    second generation (Pauline),
        47
    third generation (Pauline), vii,
        xvi, 3–4, 47–48, 68–69, 77,
        84, 90–91, 94–95, 99–101,
        105, 109
geography, 58, 74, 76, 78, 96, 123
glory, 14–18, 50
Golden Rule, 39
gospels, 28, 50, 116, 120–21
    gospel of God, 59
grace, 9, 42, 43, 98, 105, 110
grammata, 78
    grammateus, 63, 114
    grammatikos, 78
Great Harbor, 76
Greece, 33, 57, 71, 75, 85, 119
    Greek citizens, 76
    Greek culture, 13, 83, 91
    Greek (ethnic), 6, 32, 47, 76,
        80, 105, 110–11, 114, 119
    Greek (language), 5, 6, 9, 14,
        28, 32, 37, 40, 49, 58, 67, 69,
        72–79, 81, 83–87, 91, 93, 98,
        100, 102–3, 113–19, 120
    Greek translation, 4, 77, 81–82
group, 4, 6, 8, 10–11, 17–19,
    22–40, 44–47, 50–58, 64, 92, 97,
    104–8, 114–15, 121
    group/collectivity, 10–11
    group-oriented person, 41
    embedded group, 17, 38
    ethnic group, 17, 25, 27, 29,
        31–32, 44, 76, 80, 90, 113
    kinship group, 17, 27, 29–34,
        38–40, 44

fictive kinship group, 27, 29, 32, 33, 38, 40, 42
group identity, 4, 79
ingroup, 4, 23–25, 26–27, 37, 53, 57–59, 106
Jesus group, 1, 4–6, 18, 24–27, 33–38, 40–49, 51–54, 57–53, 66, 75, 82–84, 96–101, 103–9
outgroups, 57
Pauline group, 3, 105, 109
small group, 5, 103–4, 106, 117, 121–22
formation of small groups, 106
small group development, 5, 103–4, 117
social group, 36
Gruen, Erich S., 80, 115, 119
guest, 87, 97

Hades, 15
Hall, Edward T., 29, 112, 119
harmony, 16, 23, 26–27, 59, 103, 108
Harré, Rom, 11–12, 111, 119
Harris, Grace Gredys, 10, 110, 119
Hartin, Patrick J., 117, 119
Hector, 16, 24, 91
Hellenistic education, 91, 101, 102
Hellenistic period, 71
Hellenistic warrior ethos, 91
Hellenistic wisdom, 63
Hellenistic world, 4, 6, 24, 69, 77, 91, 94, 95, 101, 102
Hellenized Israelites, 4, 6, 31, 32, 58, 71, 76, 79, 80, 84, 87, 88, 95, 97
in Alexandria, 80, 89
in Corinth, 99
in Egypt, 79, 88
Jesus group, 58

Hellenized Israelite colonies, 74
community, 79, 80, 83, 85, 86, 90, 91, 94
Heptastadium, 76
Herod the Great, 74
hieroi periboloi (sacred places), 86
Higgins, Henry, 12
Hillel, Rabbi, 34
ho mathētēs, 61
Homer, 9, 15, 97, 111, 122
Homeric epics, 19
Homeric value system, 17
honor, 13, 14, 16–18, 26, 30, 50–52, 56, 86, 97, 107
honor/glory ethic, 18
Hornblower, Simon, 113, 120
hospitality, 95, 97, 117, 121
Mediterranean, 97
rules of, 97

identity, 3–5, 8, 10, 17, 24, 31, 36, 51–53, 55, 58, 79, 84, 88–90, 94, 104, 106, 111–12
dyadic identity, 52, 53
ethnic identity, 79, 84
Iliad, 13, 14, 16, 24, 91, 97, 111, 122
Index Philoneus, 116, 121
Individual, Self, Person, 9, 10
individualism, 20, 111–12, 121–22
Individualistic versus Collectivistic Cultures, 23
interpretation, 2, 18–19, 26, 34–35, 62, 83, 111–12, 119–21
Ioudaios and *Ioudaismos*, 6
Israel, 31–32, 53, 56, 69, 70–72, 74, 76, 79, 82, 84, 113, 115
house of Israel, 4, 6, 31, 38, 56, 69, 73
God of Israel, 42, 44, 56–58, 94, 98, 101

Israelites, 6, 31–32, 35, 56–57, 61, 70–71, 74, 76, 79, 81, 83–84, 86, 90–91, 99, 104–5
(*see* Hellenized Israelites)
Israelite colonies, 71, 72, 74, 75, 79, 83, 103
Israelite identity, 84, 88, 90
Israelite inscriptions, 86
Israelite theocracy, 5, 34–35, 43, 56–58, 61, 98, 101, 103, 105–6, 108–9
non-Israelites, 32, 57–58, 90
Italy, 71, 85
Ioudaios, 6, 31
Ioudaismos, 6

Jason, 33
Jerusalem, 35, 71, 73–74, 81, 86–88, 105
Jesus, xiii, xv, 5–6, 18, 28, 34–36, 39–43, 47, 50–59, 61–62, 66, 82, 95–96, 98–99, 101, 103, 105, 106, 109
Jesus as Messiah, 5, 26, 56, 57–58, 96, 98, 103
resurrected Jesus, 5, 26, 34–35, 40, 42–43, 53, 55–59, 61, 63, 96, 103, 106, 109
Jesus group, 1, 4–6, 18, 24–27, 33–38, 40–49, 51–54, 57–63, 66, 75, 82–84, 96–101, 103–9
in Corinth, 18, 24–27, 45, 99–100
in Egypt, 25, 35
in Rome, 43
John the Baptist, 53, 96, 98
John's baptism, xvi, 34, 53, 95–99
Josephus, 34, 39, 73–74, 79, 87, 122
Judea, 6, 35, 56, 69, 72, 74, 76, 83, 88–89, 96

Judean, 6, 35, 50, 57, 70, 74, 79, 105, 110
Judean and Greek, 6
Judean and Hellenist, 105, 110
Judean communities, 70
Judean leaders, 50
judicial, 93
justice, 16, 116

kardia, 15
kēr, 15
kingdom of God, 34, 51
kinship, 32, 35–36, 52, 66
(*see* group, kinship group)
kleos, 14–15
Kluckhohn, F. R., 113, 120

law, 27, 34–35, 39, 73, 81–82, 87–89, 91, 95
Israelite law, 34, 73
law of Moses, 35
oral law, 73
Letter of Aristeas, 77, 79, 81, 123
Letter of James, 41
letter of recommendation, 25, 27, 97, 98
Levine, John M., 117, 121
Levine, Lee I., 88–89, 116, 120
Liddell, Henry George, 114, 116, 120
literature, 72–74, 75, 77–78, 92
Christian literature, 113–18
Rabbinic literature, 34, 87
sacred literature, 74–75
local community, 88
locus of human experience, 10
Logos, 83
loyalty, 29, 38–41, 85–86, 104
loyalty formula, 86
Luckmann, Thomas, 112, 118
Luke, xvi, 3–4, 30, 42, 46–49, 57, 67–69, 75, 77, 95–96, 98–102, 105, 111–12, 120–21

Mack, Burton L., 92, 116, 120–21
Malina, Bruce, 5, 47–48, 50–51,
    56–57, 64, 92, 97–98, 100, 110,
    111–14, 116–17, 120–21
Marc Antony, 77
marriage, 30
mathematics, 78
Matsumoto, D., 112, 120
McKenzie, Judith, 115, 121
medical center, 78
Mediterranean world, 8, 13,
    17–19, 27–28, 30, 32, 70, 74, 77,
    79, 91, 93, 95, 97, 102, 113
    first-century Mediterranean
        culture, ix, 7, 22, 36, 49–50,
        55
    first-century Mediterranean
        person, 3, 7, 8, 20, 37, 43–44,
        69, 92, 102
    Mediterranean islands, 71
meeting places, 4
Mendels, Doron, 71, 115, 119
Menelaus, 97
mēnis, 13
Messiah, xvi, 5, 26, 34, 54, 56–59,
    96, 98–99, 103, 105
    God's Messiah, 54, 57–59,
        98–99
mind, xiii, 1, 3, 9, 15, 29, 36, 40,
    42–43, 54, 81, 85, 107, 111, 118,
    122
ministry, 25, 42, 96
Mithridates VI Eupator Dionysus,
    78
morality, 11, 23, 26, 27, 37, 38
    moral order, 12–14, 17, 19
Moreland, Richard L., 117, 121
mother-talk, 12
motivation, 23–24, 111, 122
muse, 14
Museum, 77, 91, 118
myths, 33

Nazareth, 28, 57, 87, 101
Near Eastern countries, 29
network of groups, 39
Neyrey, Jerome, 57, 92, 111–14,
    116, 120–21
Nicea, 6
Nile Delta, 76
Nitriai, 85
norming, 104–5, 106–7
    norming stage, 106–7
norms, 21, 22, 23, 26, 31, 33, 44
Nunnally, W. E., 113, 121

obedience, 23, 37, 41, 43–44
    obedience of Jesus, 42
    obedience to the law of
        Moses, 35
Odyssey, 97, 117
oikonomos, 106, 117
Orator, 92
orators, 60, 66, 69

Papajohn, John, 113, 121
papyrological manuscripts, 85
papyrus, 77
Paris, 97
partners or collaborators, 108
Passover, 88
Pastoral Letters, 26, 48, 109
patriarch, 30–31
    patriarchal father, 32–33
    patriarchal world, 30
Paul, 1, 3–6, 18, 25–27, 32–36,
    40–49, 52–69, 83, 94–95, 98–121
    Paul's social network, 1, 3, 5,
        34–36, 44–45, 47–49, 68–69,
        108, 117, 121
Pauline generation, 47–49, 67–68,
    75, 79, 81–82, 92, 94, 96, 98,
    101–2, 109
    first Pauline generation, vii, 4,
        46–49, 57, 99, 100, 109

second Pauline generation, 47
third Pauline generation,
    vii, xvi, 3–4, 47–48, 68–69,
    77, 84, 90–91, 94–95, 99–101,
    105, 109
pedagogy, 33
Pentecost, 88
performing, 93, 104
perfumes, 77
Pergamum, 78
personality, 3, 19, 21–23, 27–28,
    36, 46, 49, 100, 110–12, 114,
    116, 118, 120
Pesach, 88
Peter, 33, 40, 52, 66
Pharos, 76
Philo (of Alexandria), 5, 19, 70,
    73–74, 79, 83, 86, 94, 101–2,
    116, 121–22
philologist, 78
philosophy, 2, 78, 83, 102
    philosophical center, 78
    philosophical wisdom, 66,
        83
philotimia, 60
phrenes, 15
physics, 78
piety, 116
Pilch, John, 50–51, 55–56, 70, 98,
    110, 112–17, 120–21
pilgrimages, 88
pistis, 38, 113
Plato, 15–17, 19, 111, 123
    Platonic philosophy, 18–19,
        78, 83, 94
pogrom, 80, 87
polis, 27, 29–37, 40, 44
    non-Israelite *poleis*, 57
politeuma, 79
Poseidon's temple, 61
prayer, 74, 84–85, 88–89, 116
    place of prayer, 84, 89, 116

Priscilla and Aquila, xvi, 34–36,
    42–44, 47–48, 94, 96, 108–9
progymnasmata, 93
proseuchē, 4, 84–90, 94–95, 104, 116
    Ephesian *proseuchē*, 90
province of Asia, 95
Pseudepigrapha, 72, 74, 115, 119,
    123
psychē, 15–16
psychological attributes, 12
psychological growth/
    development, 28
psychological symbiosis, 11, 12,
    15, 18, 21, 112
psychologistic, 18–19
Ptolemy, 85, 86
    Ptolemy I, 77, 81, 85–86
    Ptolemy II Philadelphus, 77,
        81
    Ptolemy III Euergetes, 77–78,
        86
Pygmalion (My Fair Lady), 12

Qumran (the Damascus
    Document), 87
    Qumran purification rituals, 98

Rabbinic literature, 34, 87
Rakotis, 76
*Random House Webster's College
    Dictionary*, 110, 113–15
reason, 16–19
Reece, Steve, 117, 121
rejection, 12, 23, 27, 59
Republic, 16, 111, 123
reputation, 15, 34, 77–78
responsibility, 23, 27
revelations, 62
rhetoric, 62, 83, 91–93, 99–100, 109
    art of persuasion, 91
    art of rhetoric, 91–92, 93, 101
    rhetorical education, 90, 92,
        94

rhetorical eloquence, 61, 99,
100
rhetorical wisdom, 62, 101
Rhetorica, 92
Rhetorica ad Alexandrum, 92
Rhetorica ad Herennium, 92, 93
ritual baths, 73
Robbins, Vernon K., 92, 116,
120–21
Rome, 36, 43, 71, 75–76, 78
Romans, 56, 87, 96, 115, 119
Roman authorities, 50
Roman Empire, 36, 71
Roman Emperors, 80
Greco-Roman, 89, 119, 116

Sabbath, 84, 105
sacred places, 86, 116
Scott, Robert, 114, 116, 120
Scriptures, xvi, 4, 5, 18–19, 26, 32,
35, 38, 43, 62, 75, 77, 81–83, 89,
95–103, 105
Hebrew Scriptures, 77, 81–82
Israelite Scriptures, 37
Sacred Scriptures, 32, 43, 82,
89, 103
seacher, 33, 34, 61, 62, 98–99, 108
self, vii, 3–4, 7–23, 110–19, 122
concept of, 3
sense of 8, 12–20
Septuagint, 4, 72, 75, 81–83, 101,
103
shame, 30, 50, 56
honor and shame, 30, 50
Shavuot, 88
Shaw, George Bernard, 12
Silas, 48
Silent Language, 112, 119
Snell, Bruno, 111, 122
social network, ix, 1, 3, 5, 34–36,
44–45, 47–49, 59, 68–69, 108–9,
113, 115, 117, 120–21

social structure, 30–31, 119
socialization, 21, 31, 112, 117, 121
socialized, 30–31, 37–38, 41,
44
social-science, 5, 22, 92, 110,
113–14, 117, 120
social-science commentary,
110, 113–14, 117, 120
social-science methodology, 5
social-science study, 22, 92
social-scientific, 2, 4, 110, 119
society, 7–16, 18, 20–22, 24, 26,
29–31, 36, 38, 50, 91, 107, 110,
112, 118, 120
Eskimo societies, 11
Greek society, 14, 110, 118
limited goods society, 14, 18,
50
Mediterranean society, 9,
10, 15, 29
first-century Mediterra-
nean society, 11, 31
Western society, 8, 10, 12
Sociology of Knowledge, 112, 118
Socrates, 16
Sophists, 61, 123
sophos, 63
Sosthenes, xiii, 3
soul, 15–16, 18
Spawforth, Antony, 113, 120
spices, 77
Spiegel, John, 113, 121
spirit, 16, 40, 61–62, 91, 99, 100
Spirit of God, 61, 62, 99
spiritual wisdom, 62, 99, 100
state, 16
Stephen, 54, 115, 121
Stoic, 83, 94
storming, 104–6
Strabo, 96, 123
Strodtbeck, F. L., 113, 120
Sukkoth, 88

Sulla, 78
suzētētēs, 63
synagogue, xvi, 25, 27, 69, 73, 84,
    87–90, 94–96, 105, 115–16, 120
    synagogē, 103
    synagogue inscriptions, 73
syneidēsis, 37
Syria, 70, 85

Tables, 78
Tarsus, 36, 102
Taylor, Charles, 16, 111, 122
technai, 92
temenos, 86
temperance, 116
temple, 71, 73–74, 88–90, 105
    temple in Judea, 88–89
Theodotos inscription, 87, 88
Theon (*Progymnasmata*), 93
Thessalonica, 60
thymos, 15
Tiberias, 87
timē, 14
Timothy, 33, 47, 48, 104, 108–9,
    113, 117, 120
Titus, xvi, 1, 26, 47, 104, 109
Topica, 92
Torah 34, 73, 81, 87–90, 95
trade, 76
    trade guild, 33
    trade routes, 74, 96
tradition, xvii, 5, 26, 43, 76, 93,
    100
Trans-Jordan, 71
traveling Israelite, 75, 96
traveling speaker, 98
traveling teacher, 98
Triandis, Henry C., 21, 111–12,
    121–22
Troy, 24
    Trojan War, 78, 97
Tuckman, B. W., 117, 122

values, 9, 11, 14, 17–19, 21–23, 26,
    29, 31–33, 37–39, 41, 44, 46, 50,
    110, 112–13, 117–18, 121
    value system, 17, 26
    embedded values, 37
    social, 33, 117, 121
voluntary associations, 33

wandering preacher, 25
warrior, 14, 16, 18–19, 91
    society, 14
    warrior ethic, 16, 19, 91
Watson, D. F., 91, 116
Way of God, xvi, 34–35, 42, 94,
    96, 98
Way of the Lord, xvi, 34, 38,
    42–44, 62, 95, 96
Weill, Raymond, 87
Western civilization, 15
Western cultures, 4
Western Harbor, 76
Western individuals, 17
Western Mediterranean, 36, 71,
    74, 94, 103, 115
    Western Mediterranean
        colonies, 72, 74–75, 85, 87,
        89–90
Western society, 8, 10, 12
Western world, 10–12, 27, 37, 41,
    44
wisdom, xii, 33, 36, 53, 60–63,
    66–67, 69, 78, 82, 83, 99,
    100–102
worldview, 26, 41, 72

xenoi, 97

zēlos, 60
Zenas, xvi, 109
Zenodotus, 78
zeōn tō pneumati, 100
Zeus, 14, 16

SCRIPTURE AND ANCIENT
AUTHORS INDEX

Gen
24:24   30

Deut
21:23   54

Ps
146:2   114

Isa
49:6   114

Jdt
5:19   115

2 Macc
1:27   115

Sir
Prologue   114–15

Matt
4:21   30
7:12   39
18:15-17   39

Luke
8:3   30

Acts
5:34-39   34

9:1-18   54
9:2   96
13:13-52   95
13:15-16   95
13:16-17   32
15   35
16:1-5   108
17:1-10   60
17:16-34   60
18   99, 100
18:4   105
18:11   105
18:24   19, 31, 35, 69, 75, 77, 81–83, 90–92, 94, 99, 102
18:24-25   62, 98
18:24-28   xvi, 1, 34, 69, 99–100
18:25   38, 44, 62, 95–96, 100
18:25-26   42
18:26   25, 35, 84, 90, 94, 96, 98
18:27   25, 96–98
18:27-28   99, 105
22:3   33, 34

Rom
1:4-5   43
1:16   6
2:9   6
12:2   43
16:1   97

1 Cor
1:1   42
1:10   40
1:10-17   xiii, 1, 41,
                49, 52
1:10–3:23   54, 59,
                99–100
1:12   18, 59, 99
1:24   6
2:1-2   36
2:1-5   61
2:13   99
3:1-9   xiv, 1, 49
3:6   59, 103,
                105, 108
3:7   59
3:8-9   59
3:21-23   xiv, 1, 49,
                59
4:1   106
4:1-7   xiv, 1, 49
4:1-13   103, 106
16:12   xv, 1, 49,
                108

2 Cor
1:1   42
3:1   97

Gal
1:1   57
1:10-12   57
1:12   54

1:17   55
2:11   66
3:13   54
6:10   33

Phil
2:5   42
2:7-8   42
2:22   33

Col
4:10   97

1 Thess
4:1   43
4:3   43

1 Tim
3:4-5   33

Titus
2:3-10   26
3:13   xvi, 1, 109

Heb
12:1   49

Jas
5:7-11   41–42

1 Pet
5:13   33

Ancient Writers

Psalms of Solomon (PsSol)
   8:28   115

Testament of Asher (TestAsh)
   7:2   115

Dio Chrysostom

8.9	61
47.22	60
55.4-5	61

Homer

Iliad	1.1-8	14
	15.259–311	16

Josephus

Against Apion	2.38	79
	2.196	39
Vita 191		34

Philo

Embassy 281	70
Flaccus 43	79
48	116

Plato

Republic 4.441c-442d	111

Letter of Aristeas 310	79

Strabo

Geography 641–42	96
663	96